CONTENTS

PREFACE

EXPERIENCE in several underdeveloped countries has convinced me that an outsider like myself can only begin to have an appreciation of the forces shaping the social evolution or dissolution of such a country. Nevertheless, outsiders can play a useful role at the present time in interpreting that country to the richer nations of the world, provided that they do so with sympathy and tact. It is in this spirit that this little book was written, for there is not much here that will surprise Guianese who have studied their country in any depth; but it is distressing to read comments in Britain and North America, which so often misunderstand the elementary complexities of the Guianese situation.

The book is a considerable expansion of an earlier article in *Race* ('Racial Tension in British Guiana', May 1962), and I have taken the opportunity to correct some of the facts and interpretation contained in that account. There I tried to distinguish between the long-run forces which have shaped the society as it is today—particularly the physical background, the historical inheritance, and the social pressures in the community—from the more recent economic and political trends which have a more obvious impact. Within the narrow confines of an article, written hurriedly after the disturbances early in 1962, these themes suffered from lack of space for development. In the present roomier account each of these topics has a chapter to itself, although of course the small compass allowed still prevents anything like a complete analysis of the country. In particular I have provided no discussion of such important matters as constitutional development, religious issues, or problems of education and local government, for which

among much else the reader is referred to Raymond Smith's excellent *British Guiana*.[1]

In emphasising the role played by long-run forces in bringing British Guiana to its present state of hectic stagnation, I wish in no way to minimise the crucial role played by the human factor, specially that of political leadership. Rather, by trying to show both how the background forces establish a framework for the present situation and how short-run forces interact both among themselves and with the long-run forces to produce either progress or retrogression in that situation, I hope to help demonstrate just what are the conditions of, and the opportunities for, wise political leadership; and for effective assistance by the colonial power, which has so far shown every sign of being bored by the problems of British Guiana.

April 1964   PETER NEWMAN

[1] Oxford University Press for the Royal Institute of International Affairs, 1962.

PART I

THE FORCES IN THE BACKGROUND

I. GEOGRAPHY AND NATURAL RESOURCES

ALL events in British Guiana take place against a background of definite and peculiar geography, whose nature must be clearly grasped at the outset; for the form of its economic organisation—which has determined so much else—has itself been a response not only to colonial status but also to the strange physical environment. The country lies in the middle of a large, ancient and relatively homogeneous region which consists also of Dutch Guiana (Surinam) and French Guiana, together with the northern marches of Brazil and the eastern part of Venezuela. The simple name Guianas, which is of Amerindian origin and is reputed to mean 'Lands of Waters', is often used for the whole of this vast area, whose rough boundaries are the River Amazon on the east and south, the Rio Negro—Rio Branco system to south and west, the Orinoco on west and northwest, and the Atlantic Ocean elsewhere. British Guiana itself lies due south of Newfoundland and faces well out into the Atlantic; the Caribbean, to which newspaper accounts often consign it, does not begin until Trinidad, a few hundred miles to the west. It is often forgotten that very nearly the whole of South America lies *east* of Florida.

The 'Lands of Waters' are well-named, for the region receives a heavy rainfall and is full of great rivers. Apart from the enormous basins of the Amazon, Negro and

Orinoco (which are of course fed from other parts of the
continent as well), there are many big rivers which flow
from south to north through the Guianas, some tumbling
down off the Pakaraima Mountains which lie in the southeast of Venezuela and the west of B.G.[1] (such streams as the
Cuyuni and Potaro), and others which come down much
more gently from the lower ancient tablelands in the south,
including the great Essequibo, the Demerara, the Berbice,
the Corentyne and the Marowijne, the last river lying
between Surinam and French Guiana. All the rivers flow
broadly through rather low-lying forest land (though with
occasional rapids) on their way to their destination in the
Atlantic, finally emerging on the mudflats that border the
brown sea. There are no golden beaches. The estuaries
contain much river-borne silt, and in fact the coast itself
consists mainly of clays that have been built up from
alluvial deposits originating in the Amazon delta and carried
westwards for hundreds of miles by ocean currents. The
natural vegetation of the coast is mangrove swamp, but over
very long stretches—at least in B.G.—this swamp has been
reclaimed at great cost in human labour and converted to
fertile sugar-cane and rice lands, which lie mostly below
sea level and so need protection, in Dutch fashion, by a sea
wall.

In area British Guiana is a large country by the standards
of the West Indies, and is not really small even when
measured on a world scale. Its 83,000 square miles make
it about the size of Great Britain and dwarf the areas of
Jamaica, Trinidad and Tobago, and Barbados, which are
4411, 1980 and 163 square miles respectively. But only the
coastal strip is of any social and economic importance, for
on it lives ninety per cent of the population, over half a
million people. Crowded onto an occupied area of only
about a thousand square miles, these people give rise to a
population density comparable with those of most of the

[1] This abbreviation is standard in British Guiana, and it will often be
used here.

West Indian islands. Indeed from many points of view the coastland of British Guiana *is* a West Indian sugar island, perched at the edge of the continent and separated from the dense forest of the South American 'mainland' by the backland swamps that mark the barrier between the Amazonian clays and the white sand soils, which are derived from the pre-Cambrian Guiana Shield itself.

Five Regions of British Guiana

It is convenient to analyse the geography of B.G. by dividing it into five areas, based partly on geology and partly on other physical features, though other classifications could be and have been made. A basic dichotomy is that already mentioned, between the coastlands and the low-lying broken hilly country of the white sands that lies behind them. The coastal belt itself is about fifteen to twenty miles in width, though not uniformly so. Of this a band of about five to eight miles immediately adjacent to the sea is generally under cultivation, from the western side of the great estuary of the Essequibo to the Corentyne; the remaining belt of ten to twelve miles or so is taken up by the barrier swamps, and by the water conservancies which serve to irrigate the cultivated areas.

With much of the coastland below sea level, crossed by large rivers and resting on a high water table, problems of drainage and flood control are severe. On one side the sea has to be kept out at high tides, and on the other side the swamp waters have to be kept back at times of flood. The threat from the Atlantic is met by a sea wall, equipped with sluices through which water is pumped out at low tide, and that from the swamps by a complicated system of dykes and canals, some of which serve for irrigation and others for transport of cane in the sugar estates.

The estates, generally rectangular in shape, run back from the sea wall or from the river banks for some 5 or 6 miles until they meet the swamps, and are divided into long sections by main canals

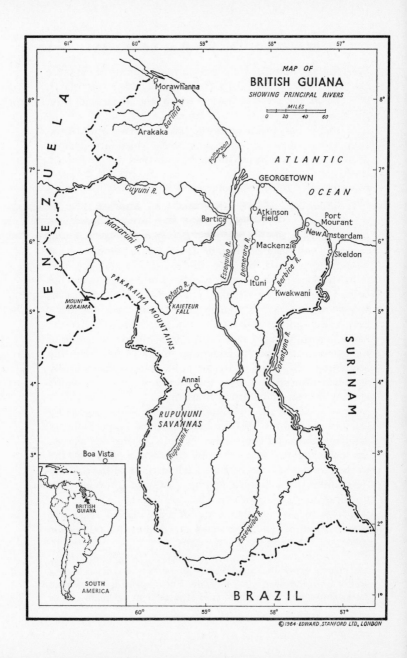

MAP OF
BRITISH GUIANA
SHOWING PRINCIPAL RIVERS

MILES
0 20 40 60

ATLANTIC

OCEAN

GEORGETOWN
Atkinson Field
Port Mourant
New Amsterdam
Bartica
Mackenzie
Skeldon
Ituni
Kwakwani

VENEZUELA

Morawhanna
Barima R.
Arakaka
Pomeroon R.
Cuyuni R.
Mazaruni R.
PAKARAIMA MOUNTAINS
MOUNT RORAIMA
Potaro R.
KAIETEUR FALL
Essequibo R.
Demerara R.
Berbice R.
Corentyne R.

SURINAM

Annai
RUPUNUNI SAVANNAS
Rupununi R.
Boa Vista
Essequibo R.

BRITISH GUIANA

SOUTH AMERICA

BRAZIL

© 1964 EDWARD STANFORD LTD., LONDON

61° 60° 59° 58° 57°
8°
7°
6°
5°
4°
3°
2°
1°

running on two levels. The higher, the irrigation and transport canals, cross the lower level drainage canals by means of aqueducts. Since the land rises less than six inches in a mile, and since the soil consists of heavy impermeable clay, the total rainfall on the estates, something between 90 and 130 inches per annum, must find its way or be led into the drainage canals and thence to the sea wall. On some estates it can finally be drained out through the sluices at low water—on most, however, it has to be pumped through them into the sea . . . It gives some idea of the extent of the estate waterways to say that each of the larger estates has some 250 miles of irrigation and transport and some 80 miles of drainage canals. They were originally dug by hand . . . maintenance is an expensive item—trenches [canals] left to themselves rapidly silt up and become choked with lotus lily or water hyacinth—an attractive sight but not appreciated by the sugar planter.[2]

Most of these private drainage systems have taken as their unit of operation the original 'estates' of around 2000 acres,[3] though the process of merger and consolidation over time has now produced much larger plantations, the average estate having around 7000 acres under cane alone. Recent Government drainage schemes, which have been designed mainly to bring land into rice cultivation, have constructed their drainage systems on a much larger scale, and no doubt the sugar estates will also move gradually in this direction as time goes on. But even the present smaller unit requires an enormous capital outlay, which is of course compensated by the sustained high fertility of the coastal soils, at least for sugar. It does mean, however, that unlike the situation in most of the West Indian islands—for example in Jamaica —no small-scale peasant farmer can hope to grow cane

[2] L. Hares: 'Field Routine', pp. 27–8 in *Bookers Sugar* (Bookers, George-town, 1954), p. 126. This glossy publication was a defence of the policies of the dominant sugar firm of Bookers, and appeared soon after the con-stitutional crisis of 1953; it contains interesting technical information about the sugar industry.

[3] See Raymond T. Smith: *British Guiana* (London, Oxford University Press for the Royal Institute of International Affairs, 1962), p. 5. This is the best modern treatment of British Guiana and its problems, especially on the social side.

successfully under Guianese conditions except in association with some large institution, such as a sugar estate, a co-operative or the Government itself, which could build and finance the expensive drainage systems required. As a result there are pitifully few peasant cane farmers, an important point to which we will return.

In and around the swampy backlands of the coastal strip there occur areas of peat soils, locally known as *pegasse*, which because of excessive acidity are relatively infertile compared to the clays, though the estates use them a little even for cane. Such soils are also found in the valleys of the second region of B.G., which is that of the white sands, beginning around the Pomeroon River just west of the Essequibo and continuing eastwards to the Corentyne and beyond, into Surinam, where the same formation is known as the Zanderij. This white sand belt is of variable width, but is usually at least eighty to one hundred miles wide; it is very infertile—the soil is almost pure quartz sand—but nevertheless supports a dense hardwood forest, chiefly because the trees are usually surface feeders which with their widespreading roots take in the organic matter left by the decay of the fallen leaves and flowers. In such conditions indiscriminate removal of the forest cover would result in barren land.

The white sands are significant mainly because they contain the most extensive bauxite deposits yet known in B.G., as well as in Surinam. The Guianese deposits occur in an inner belt of country about fifteen miles wide extending from the Pomeroon to the Corentyne, but are not uniformly distributed, being found in patches such as those around Mackenzie and Ituni. This occurrence within a curved belt (which extends into Surinam) together with other evidence has suggested strongly that the deposits may be associated with an ancient shoreline.[4]

[4] See *Report on the Geological Survey Department for the Year 1959* (George-town, Government Printers, 1960), p. 17.

The bauxite mines themselves are found in three places: south of the alumina plant at Mackenzie, which is a company town lying sixty-five miles up the Demerara from Georgetown, and is the second largest town in B.G., hewed out of the surrounding rain-forest; at Ituni, thirty-five miles southeast of Mackenzie; and at Kwakwani, which is seventy miles up the Berbice River. The first two mines are operated by the Demerara Bauxite Company, a subsidiary of the Aluminium Company of Canada, and produce about 85 per cent of the total bauxite output of some two and a half million tons, an output which makes B.G. one of the world's leading producers; the balance is mined by Reynolds Metals at Kwakwani and processed (but not into alumina) at Everton near New Amsterdam.

The remaining three regions of the country can be dealt with rather more quickly, since as yet they play no significant role in its economy, though potentially at least two of them could do so. The first of these regions is that of the northwest, lying roughly between the Mazaruni River on the south, the Venezuelan border on the north and west and the Atlantic on the north and east. Like most of the country's interior this is heavily forested with predominantly poor soils lying over heavily weathered basement rocks, in which there is some evidence of mineral wealth. The most important of these minerals at present is manganese ore, which is mined by an American company (a subsidiary of Union Carbide) around Arakaka on the Barima River not far from the Venezuela border, and which is shipped by a specially built railway to a new port near Morawhanna.

The next area is the Guianese portion of the Sierra Pakaraima lying along the borders with Venezuela and Brazil (the highest point of the whole range, Mount Roraima at 8635 feet, is at the junction of all three countries), and contained roughly within the line of rivers Mazaruni, Potaro, Essequibo and the northern part of the Rupununi. Highly inaccessible, composed of sharply stepped plateaus rising from the plain, this area is scarcely

known at all. A few Amerindian tribes live in the up-country savannas, but otherwise it is quite empty. Most of it is heavily forested, and there are many high waterfalls where the rivers suddenly spill off the plateaus on to the plain; the highest of these, Kaietur Falls on the Potaro, is—at 741 feet—over twice as high as Victoria Falls and more than four times the height of Niagara. The potential of such falls, or of any of the rivers, for hydro-electric development has not really been investigated, and nor has the possibility of mineral wealth in any detail, although there has long been gold and diamond mining (by colourful prospectors known locally as 'pork-knockers') in the streams of the foothills.

Such geological investigations as have been made are of considerable promise, revealing the existence of vast quantities of ferruginous bauxites, i.e. alumina ores containing high percentages—around 20 per cent-30 per cent—of iron oxides. There are large amounts in other areas of B.G. as well so that, taken together, it 'can claim to have tonnages of this material equal to or greater than any other country of equivalent size in the world'.[5] Unfortunately the alumina content is too low for current reduction processes, while there is too much alumina for use in conventional iron and steel works, so that the material is not of economic interest at the present time, especially in view of its inaccessibility. But it is by no means impossible that current research will produce a method of recovering both the alumina and iron, and in that event 'it is perhaps not too fanciful to imagine an industrial complex exploiting these low-grade ores with the help of British Guiana's great hydro-electric potential'.[6]

The last region is the south of British Guiana, below the 'waist' which lies at 4° North. The geology of this region is

[5] J. H. Bateson: 'Preliminary Report on the Ferruginous Bauxites of the Pakaraima Mountains', *Mineral Resources Pamphlet No. 10*, (Geological Survey Department, Georgetown, 1961), p. 2.
[6] R. B. McConnell (Director, B.G. Geological Survey) in Foreword to Bateson, op. cit.

similar in many respects to that of the northwest, but is even less known in detail. The more important part of the area at present is the Rupununi Savannas, which lie at about 250 feet above sea level on either side of the Rupununi River; they are an eastern extension of rather similar savanna areas across the border in the Rio Branco district of Brazil, whose capital is Boa Vista. To the Guianese of the coast, the Rupununi Savannas are the area of the interior which is probably best known to them, or at least the area about which the greatest myths have developed. To many of those of the coast the possibility of 'a road to the Rupununi' is the epitome of all that half-attraction, half-horror with which they regard the task of developing the interior of their country.

Yet at present only low-density cattle ranching (about one animal per seventy acres[7]) and balata collection form the chief cash activities of the region, which supports a few thousand Amerindians and some ranchers of mixed European–Amerindian ancestry; and what soil surveys have been done indicate that not much more can be expected without heavy and very expensive application of fertilisers. Moreover there appears to be small probability of mineral wealth, unlike the other areas of the interior. With these facts in mind it is difficult to understand why the Rupununi should have such a hold on the popular coastal imagination. Perhaps the absence there of heavy forest, with the lessened need for clearing and the accompanying dream of pastoral harmony, has something to do with it; perhaps not. Whatever the reasons, it would seem that other inland areas have better prospects of long-term development than this.

[7] Soil and Land-Use Surveys, No. 2: *British Guiana—The Rupununi Savannas* (Regional Research Centre, Imperial College of Tropical Agriculture, Trinidad, March 1958), p. 11. An interesting hypothesis contained in this pessimistic report is that originally the Rupununi Savannas were covered with white sand soils, identical with those closer to the coast, but that over time these have been weathered away, leaving 'a resurrected fossil landscape' (p. 15) of very low inherent fertility. The evidence cited in support of this view seems very plausible.

The Problem of Natural Resources

In a very real sense natural resources are created by man, for not only is man's technology required in order to locate and utilise the material in question, but also the very concept of a 'resource' implies that it is useful, which is to say that the current state of technology can find a place for it. Thus recent developments in the techniques of oil and gas exploration have helped to locate a very large natural gas field in Holland, a country which few people dreamed could contain petroleum or anything like it in significant quantities;[8] similarly the enormous Athabaska tar sands in Canada are not at present 'resources', though as time goes on and the techniques of their utilisation develop, while oil supplies become more difficult to obtain, they should prove a valuable source of energy.

This reasoning applies with special force to British Guiana. How rich in natural resources really is the interior? This is a question that is often asked on the coast, and the answer is that nobody really knows, partly because the terrain offers particular difficulty to geological exploration and partly because—as in the case of the iron-laden bauxites of the Pakaraimas—present metallurgical techniques are not adapted to use much of the material that is known to be present. The ancient character of much of the basement rock and the strong leaching action of the heavy rainfall have combined to reduce greatly the amount of outcropping of mineral rocks in the interior, and so to make the geologist's task more difficult. Moreover the dense forest cover both hides what is available and makes transport difficult, forcing reliance until recently on the rivers. On these travelling was slow, uncertain and hazardous, the 263 miles from Bartica at the mouth of the Essequibo to

[8] Present indications are that the mainland of British Guiana is unlikely to contain oil in any economic quantity, but there is quite a possibility that oil might be found offshore, in a belt which is more or less a geological continuation of the fields in the Gulf of Paria between Trinidad and Venezuela; but offshore drilling is expensive.

Annai on the Rupununi taking twenty to thirty days and only then at times of flood; even so it was common to lose both boat and crew on the cataracts.[9]   In recent years, however, air transport has made prospecting easier, both to convoy geologists inland (though away from the landing strips the going is still rough), and to make aerial photographic surveys.

The difficulties that apply to finding mineral wealth apply equally to the search for fertile soils and to the exploration of the potential for hydro-electric development. The prevailing expert opinion with regard to land in the interior seems to be that most of it is infertile, but that there are probably substantial patches, aggregating a considerable area, which with adequate fertilisers could produce reasonably respectable crops, though difficulties of access may preclude the early development of much of a cash agriculture in such areas.[10]

There is little doubt that opposition from coastal interests, particularly from the electricity and bauxite companies, has helped to prevent the close investigation of the possibilities of hydro-electricity.[11]   In spite of much talk, very little has actually been done to measure the potentials of the great rivers and such reports as have been produced—by the chief bauxite company, which has a giant aluminium smelter in Canada anyway—have been pessimistic.   Yet in neighbouring Surinam there is at Brokopondo, south of Paramaribo, a hydro-electric scheme of 150 megawatt capacity well on its way to completion by 1965, while other rivers there have been investigated with favourable results, including a preliminary study of the Corentyne.   It would be surprising if rather similar results could not be

[9] Soil and Land-Use Surveys, No. 2, op. cit., p. 12.
[10] See Soil and Land-Use Surveys, No. 6, *British Guiana* (Regional Research Centre, Imperial College of Tropical Agriculture, Trinidad, June 1959), Part 3, 'General Remarks'.
[11] See the interesting personal account by A. P. Thorne: 'Some Reflections on British Guiana', *Social and Economic Studies*, Vol. 12, June 1963, especially pp. 215–6.

obtained from an investigation of the rivers in British Guiana, which generally have similar hydrological régimes.

The broad picture of the economic potential of the interior is one of substantial promise, at least enough promise to warrant the mounting of vigorous surveys of the mineral, agricultural and hydro-electric possibilities. Added to the much better known—and enormous—timber resources, there is a distinct possibility that some kind of industrial complex would be at least technically feasible; at any rate it seems worth a try, for a small such grouping is already coming into being in Surinam around Paramaribo–Brokopondo, while a much larger industrial complex is being built in the Venezuelan part of Guiana, centred on Ciudad Bolivar and organised by the State-run Corporación Venezolana de Guayana.

But here we come upon a basic difficulty that confronts anyone concerned with economic development in British Guiana. Most of the projects needed to harness her natural resources effectively will have to be on a large scale, since the physical features of the country, especially the rivers, are on a large scale. Therefore much of the investment and expertise required for those projects must come in large discontinuous chunks, and these are too large for the very limited resources of the small, crowded West Indian island that occupies the coastal mudflats. For example, the cost of Surinam's Brokopondo hydro-electric installation, and of the associated aluminium smelter, is of the order of British Guiana's entire national income (about £50 million), and is quite beyond Surinam's own resources. Unless one has financial support such as massive revenues from oil (as in the case of Venezuela), then these large projects must be financed from outside, either by giant private concerns (in Surinam's case, the Aluminum Company of America), or by international aid agencies, or by foreign Governments.

The first alternative runs the real risk of having the small society dominated by one large firm and is not attractive to B.G., most of whose people vote for avowedly socialist

parties and which has had the dominant firm of Bookers in its midst for a very long time. The second possibility would be more acceptable, but unfortunately money on this kind of scale is not easily forthcoming from international institutions, especially when the small population and lack of appropriate experience in the country means that most of the skilled personnel needed for the projects would have to be imported as well. The final choice, that of loans and grants from foreign Governments, is not a very strong possibility in view of the magnitudes involved, and in any case poses basic questions of sovereignty which a small country striving for independence would (and should) naturally look at askance, regardless of which side in the cold war the money comes from.

The root of the dilemma is that the inhabited region of British Guiana is the coastland, which has been developed mainly as a sugar island; and sugar islands possess neither the skilled manpower nor the finance nor the powers of organisation required to embark on the Tennessee-Valley-type schemes that will be needed to develop the interior effectively. It would be desirable if one such scheme could be started on a fairly small scale, in a part of the interior close to the coast, so that the society could gradually learn from experience in these often difficult though rewarding ventures; but even such a modest leap across the backland swamps would probably be expensive and require supplementation by considerable outside help.

Until the last fifteen years or so the sugar estates never really had enough labour and always tried hard to dissuade the population from leaving the coast, an attempt that resulted in rather a 'coastal mentality' among the population. Coupled with the uncertainty and the large investments associated with interior development, it is not surprising that this resulted in a concentration of almost all State-supported economic development on the coastal plains, where conditions were not so strange nor on quite such a large scale. But even here, as will be argued in detail in the chapter on

the economy, there has been surprisingly little diversification into lines of activity other than the traditional sugar and rice. In part this is due to lack of technical knowledge of what can and should be done, in part perhaps to a tendency to rely overmuch on the advice of visiting experts, which is sometimes superficial and contradictory. For example, in one passage (p. 148) of the International Bank's Report[12] it was stated that 'improvements needed to increase local rice production are more of an intensive nature (yield per acre) than extensive (expansion of acreage)', while less than thirty pages on we find that 'the process of agricultural intensification cannot proceed rapidly . . . the principal contribution must come through expansion of the cultivable area' (p. 187).

A major problem in giving advice to any country is that there is an ever present danger, to be avoided only by his constant vigilance and humbleness, that the 'expert' will transfer advice quite appropriate for one country (with which he is familiar) to another where the conditions may be considerably different, although at first sight they may not appear to be so. An interesting example where this was avoided, is the following:

the heavy, generally badly drained soils in which cacao is found [in Surinam] are such a contrast to the 'deep well-drained friable loams' which agriculturists usually recommend that it is surprising that the cacao tree does so well in Surinam. The Mission saw trees 40 and 50 years old—witch-broom infected, it is sad to add—and there is no doubt that the tree grows well on the coastal plain. Its root systems have adapted themselves to a heavy clay, with barely two to three feet of dry soil in the dry season above the permanently wet zone which we may crudely call a 'water table'. Instead of the normal, long main tap root, the cacao tree here sends out fairly strong laterals with numerous fibrous roots, or has a root system composed almost entirely of a net of

[12] International Bank for Reconstruction and Development: *The Economic Development of British Guiana* (The Johns Hopkins Press, Baltimore, 1953).

fibrous roots. In those cases where deeper roots had penetrated the water table, the roots had died.[13]

This example is not without relevance to British Guiana, for the coastal plains of Surinam are more or less identical with those of B.G., where it is often claimed that cocoa does not do well on the impermeable clays. Even for the relatively easier problems of the coast, economic development—as always—requires the continued exercise of imagination and ingenuity if it is to be effective, and a constant refusal to take 'no' for an answer. The same qualities will be required in even greater measure for development of the interior.

---

[13] International Bank for Reconstruction and Development: *Surinam— Recommendations for a Ten Year Development Plan* (The Johns Hopkins Press, Baltimore, 1952), p. 134.

II. THE HISTORICAL BACKGROUND

In order to understand the present position fully, it is necessary to gain some impression of British Guiana's past, and the following few pages have been written to serve that purpose. In no sense are they meant as anything more than a summary of rather well-known facts about the country, and so few attempts are made to cite the sources of information. Emphasis is placed on economic and social history rather than on constitutional developments, which are readily accessible elsewhere.[1]

The Early Period

In his third voyage to the Americas in 1498, which was to end so disastrously in his being sent back to Spain in irons, Columbus sailed on a more southerly route than usual, passing along the coast of the Guianas and then through the Gulf of Paria between Venezuela and Trinidad to the island of Margarita, before striking northwestward to his base in Hispaniola. But in spite of this early reconnaissance the Guianas—unlike Trinidad and Jamaica—did not become part of the Spanish settlements, perhaps because the mangrove-lined shores of this 'Wild Coast' did not seem inviting compared to the excitements of Cuba and Mexico and the countries of the Andes. It was left to Raleigh and other English and Dutch captains one hundred years later

[1] See R. Smith, op. cit., Chapters II, III and VII, who bases his account of the earlier period (up to 1928) on the standard work by Sir Cecil Clementi, *A Constitutional History of British Guiana* (Macmillan, London, 1937). Smith's two earlier chapters also contain a good brief discussion of most of the other aspects of Guiana's history. A very useful elementary account for the general reader is contained *passim* in *The Making of the West Indies* by F. R. Augier, S. C. Gordon, D. G. Hall and M. Reckord (Longmans, London, 1960). Their Chapter 17 on 'Immigrant Workers' is especially well done at this level and highly relevant to the Guianese situation. An older and very full history is James Rodway: *History of British Guiana from 1668* (Georgetown, 1891–1894), three volumes.

to explore these coasts in their quest for El Dorado, the legendary empire of gold. Unlike the Spaniards in Mexico City and Cuzco, these northerners found nothing resembling the golden city of Manoa, the fabled capital of El Dorado, for the Guianas were sparsely settled by rather backward and nomadic Indian tribes, whose lives were based either on hunting and fishing or on a primitive agriculture; no trace of any Indian culture anywhere nearly so advanced as that of the Incas has yet been found in the Guianas.

In England and Holland the accounts published by the returning explorers stimulated interest in this non-Iberian part of South America, and several plans for settlement were projected in the first decades of the seventeenth century, even the Pilgrim Fathers giving Guiana serious consideration before wisely deciding to make for New England. Many unsuccessful attempts were made to establish colonies in this inhospitable area, and it was not until 1616 that a group of Dutch and English settlers, under Dutch leadership, founded a secure colony on an island in the estuary of the Essequibo; a little earlier, in 1613, the French had landed at what is now Cayenne in French Guiana, and a little later an entirely English settlement was created in Surinam, so that British Guiana was originally Dutch, and Dutch Guiana originally British.

The Dutch colonies in Essequibo later extended to Demerara, although the settlement of Berbice was a quite separate undertaking, the two groups not being united until 1831,[2] long after Britain had taken full control of the whole area in 1803. Encouraged by the Dutch West India Company, the early Dutch settlements were at least as interested in trade with the Indian tribes as they were in the production of commodities, and to this end established a trading network far up into the interior even as far as the Rupununi. For the growing of crops, which at that early time included

[2] See Rawle Farley: 'The Unification of British Guiana', *Social and Economic Studies*, Vol. 4, June 1955, pp. 168–183, for an account of the reasons why.

tobacco, cotton, coffee and cocoa but not sugar, they cultivated the lands lining the banks of the rivers, for many miles
upstream. These were much easier to bring into cultivation
than the swamps of the coast, and were considerably more
secure from attacks by roving privateers.

As time went on the need for increased labour to work
the plantations began to be felt. Very few of the original
inhabitants were willing to work and the early attempts to
rely mainly on European labour came to nothing, as the
climate and internal squabbles drove many of the early
settlors to Barbados and the Lesser Antilles, many of whose
islands were first colonised by Europeans from the Guianas.
As in the rest of the Americas, this need for labour was met
by the importation of slaves, some of whom came from
other slave lands in the New World, but most of whom came
more or less direct from West Africa.

During the course of the eighteenth century a number of
developments began to work themselves into a pattern, a
pattern of which a great deal persists today. First, although
the whole area continued under Dutch sovereignty[3] there
was an increasing flow of British and other colonists, many
of them from the West Indian islands (especially Barbados)
so that British influence became increasingly important.
This was especially so when the great Commandeur of
Essequibo and Demerara, Laurens Storm van 's Graven-
sande, in 1746 threw open the Demerara region to settlement with promises of free land and exemption from poll-
tax for ten years. By 1760 the British were more numerous
than the Dutch in Demerara (and of course Negroes far
more numerous than either).

Secondly, there was a gradual shift away from those crops
that we have mentioned, as other areas in the world were

[3] In addition to the three colonies of Essequibo, Demerara and Berbice,
the Dutch also by then controlled Surinam, which was ceded to them at
the Treaty of Breda in 1667 in exchange for what is now New York
State; with due respect to Surinam it would seem that the British had
the better of the deal.

developed which could produce these commodities (or their close rivals) far more easily and cheaply, as in the case of tobacco and cotton in what became the Southern States of the U.S.A. The crop which was increasingly favoured in the Guianas was sugar, which was first grown in a Pomeroon settlement in 1658, and which slowly came to assume the dominant position in Essequibo and Demerara, though not in Berbice which for a long time grew coffee and cotton to the exclusion of almost everything else.

The third strand in development, which was intimately connected with the second factor, was the gradual move of the estates from the banks of the rivers (where they were located as far as fifty miles inland) to the coastal strip, where they have remained ever since. This process has apparently never been fully analysed, but is probably best accounted for by the considerably diminished attractiveness of the river lands and the increased profitability of the coastal strip. The riverain lands were usually cultivated without any attempt to maintain their fertility, and as this decreased the planters naturally shrank from opening up the dense forest away from the rivers, especially as their soils were not very good either, and the crops for which they were suited were coming under increasing competition from elsewhere. That was one side of the coin; the other was the trend to sugar, for which the coastal clays were ideally suited once they had been drained and irrigated; and the Dutch of course were especially good at the control of low-lying lands. Moreover after the Treaty of Utrecht in 1713 there was greatly increased security in the area, and the coast became a safer place to live in and to develop.

So gradually the river lands were abandoned and all cultivation confined to the coast, and most of the other crops were considerably reduced, the emphasis being placed on sugar, particularly after the British occupation in 1803. From about 1810 onwards British Guiana began to be a significant exporter of sugar on a world scale, just as Jamaica entered into her decline. In 1812 Demerara

produced about 11,400 tons of sugar and 7.7 million lbs. of
coffee; by 1833 she was producing 36,800 tons of sugar and
only 4.3 million lbs. of coffee.[4] In fact at this period, as
Ragatz in particular has pointed out,[5] Trinidad and British
Guiana constituted a kind of rapidly expanding West
Indian 'frontier', in the American sense of that term.
Production rose rapidly, slave prices were the highest in the
British possessions, and for most of the time profits were
quite satisfactory.

A switch to sugar and to the coastlands had very important consequences for the structure of the society and of the
economy in B.G. Even in the sugar islands, where generally
there were few of the drainage and irrigation problems that
beset the Guianese colonists, the victory of sugar over the
other crops meant a considerable increase in the size of the
average plantation, for cane cultivation is (or at least was)
extensive rather than intensive, requires the use of a good
deal of transport equipment and of processing machinery,
and needs large groups of workmen, both in the field and the
factory. Nowadays these disadvantages of scale are often
met partly by informal or formal co-operatives, in which
the peasant producer sends his cane to a central factory for
milling. But in that period there were no peasants, only
slaves, and the social organisation did not permit the
decentralisation of sugar production. Therefore even in the
islands the change to sugar forced a much larger and more
capitalistic type of operation on the planters, and as one
consequence they became much more dependent on
merchants and banks for the supply of fixed and working
capital. The consequences of sugar for the type of society in
the islands, with their large agglomerations of unskilled
slave labour often living in unspeakable conditions, are too
well known to need development here.

[4] Augier *et al.*, p. 120 and p. 122.
[5] L. J. Ragatz: *The Fall of the Planter Class in the British Caribbean, 1763–
1833* (Oxford University Press, 1928), p. 332.

All these implications of sugar's dominance were seen in a heightened form on the B.G. coastlands, where the nature of the terrain made the advantages of large-scale operation in sugar even more pronounced than in the islands. Moreover since the Guianese plantations came on the world sugar scene at a rather late stage compared to most of the islands, they were able to install the latest—and most costly— milling equipment, which put them at a competitive advantage compared to such places as Barbados, which continued with old-fashioned 'muscovado' sugars for far too long. These factors worked together to make sugar production in B.G. a very capitalistic enterprise, with considerable dependence on creditors of all kinds, and therefore particularly susceptible to the swings of fortune. The dependence on an adequate supply of labour was complete, for there was not then—as there is now—a possibility of machinery being able to substitute for any but a very few of the arduous tasks in the fields and the trenches. Preoccupation with the need to maintain a plentiful labour force for the coastal estates was constant throughout the nineteenth century and well into the twentieth, especially since the estates with their miles of near-stagnant water were often unhealthy places in which to live and work, in some cases being so bad that their populations were unable to maintain themselves, let alone to increase.

Emancipation and After

The advent first of the period of 'apprenticeship' in 1834 and then of full slave emancipation exactly four years later changed the whole basis of sugar production in British Guiana, and its adverse effects on profits were greatly enhanced by the increasing difficulty that all the West Indies had in selling sugar on the British market, when preferential duties for Empire sugar were abolished in the period 1846 to 1854, a move that was followed by the lowering of general sugar tariffs in England, finally achieving

completely free trade in 1874. These two factors—the
scarcity of labour causing pressure on the supply side and
the abolition of preferences causing difficulties of demand—
acted and reacted on each other in the twenty years or so
following apprenticeship to give the sugar planters a
difficult time. Sugar production was fairly stationary until
the late eighteen fifties, prices fell, wages rose and so there
was considerable pressure for the closing or consolidation
of estates, as many planters fell into the hands of merchant
creditors. It was in this way that the present-day giant of
Bookers began to gain control of the B.G. sugar industry; it
was originally a Liverpool merchant firm which gained
possession of a local supply firm and then, as estates went
bankrupt, went into plantation ownership. At the end of
the eighteenth century there were 380 estates on the coast,
in 1829 just before apprenticeship there were 230, in 1849
180, and—as a result also of other difficulties later in the
nineteenth century—by 1896 there were only 64. Today
there are twelve separate estate administrations, of which
ten are controlled by Bookers and the other two by the
Demerara Company.[6]

The compensation per slave paid to the Guianese
planters at emancipation was the highest of all the British
slave territories, and in itself indicated the relative scarcity
of workers on the coast estates. As Augier *et alii* have
pointed out, the reaction of ex-slaves to the new situation
was different in different countries, depending chiefly on
whether there was cultivable land available either free or
at a reasonable price, on to which they could move and set
up as peasants. In Barbados, St. Kitts and Antigua there
was no land available but in Trinidad and British Guiana
there certainly was, as there was in many parts of Jamaica.
With no spare land the freed slaves were forced to stay tied

[6] See Appendix A of E. P. Reubens and B. G. Reubens: *Labour Displace-
ment in a Labour-Surplus Economy: The Sugar Industry of British Guiana*
(Institute of Social and Economic Research, University of the West
Indies, Jamaica, 1963), pp. 94–5.

as wage-labour to the sugar estates, but elsewhere there was a choice, and always they chose to be peasants; the memories of slavery, and of the severe way in which uprisings had been treated, were not such as to recommend the other course. In British Guiana there was considerable fear by the planters that the freemen would migrate far into the bush of the interior, which they had been prevented by force from doing to any significant extent in the time of slavery (there is a contrast here with the so-called Bush Negroes of Surinam, who survive as a culture quite separate from the rest of the country). But there was no move at all in this direction, for the general desire was to stay on the coast, usually on already abandoned plantations or on others that the owners were willing to sell; a common pattern was for quite a large group of freemen to band together to buy an estate,[7] which they then divided among themselves, thus forming co-operative 'villages' whose sense of unity was very strong,[8] and which became the nuclei of local government organisation.

However the new coastal peasantry were not successful in finding a commercial crop, especially an export crop which would yield them the cash income that, supplemented by the subsistence crops which they grew, would give a satisfactory livelihood. The reasons why they were not likely to be successful in sugar have already been discussed in the last chapter, and probably similar factors of drainage and irrigation, together with the whole orientation of the trading community to sugar, made it difficult to export other cash crops such as cocoa and coffee. This may be contrasted with the situation in Jamaica, where the peasantry were much more successful—partly for reasons of geography, partly because of the greater size of the whole economy—in

[7] See Rawle Farley: 'The Rise of the Peasantry in British Guiana', *Social and Economic Studies*, Vol. 2, 1954.
[8] For evidence of how this solidarity persists today, especially in matters of ownership, see R. T. Smith: 'Land Tenure in Three Villages in British Guiana', *Social and Economic Studies*, Vol. 4, 1955, pp. 64–82.

becoming truly independent operators, especially after the rise of the banana industry in the eighteen seventies. Thus the Guianese Negroes did not divorce themselves wholly from the sugar economy, but continued in general to provide part-time help in the field and the factory, and in the various commercial firms in the towns that depended directly or indirectly on the sugar trade.

But this part-time help was neither large enough nor certain enough to sustain the sugar economy completely, at a period when in order to maintain income in the face of weakened prices it felt it had to make every effort to increase production. At no time was there any serious thought given to the idea that B.G. would be better off as a country of independent peasants without a sugar plantation industry. Even the more altruistic members of the Colonial Office, who regarded themselves as agents for the welfare of the freemen against the West Indian Interest, could see no other solution than the active support of the sugar industry. As Lord Harris, the Governor of Trinidad, wrote to the Secretary of State in words that could apply unchanged to the official attitude in B.G.:

I fully and cordially agree with you that the highest interest of the negroes requires that the cultivation of sugar should not be abandoned, and that the proprietors of European race should be enabled to maintain their present place in the society of the colony, which can only be done by giving them greater command of labour.[9]

Since the British authorities held with equal principle (or if one prefers, with equal hypocrisy) to the cheap sugar yielded by freer trade and were not prepared to revert to preferential duties, the only help they could give was on the supply side, by helping the planters find an adequate labour supply; and this they did by giving financial assistance for the immigration of indentured labour.

[9] Quoted by Augier *et al.* op cit., p. 201.

Soon after the 'apprenticeship' scheme began in 1834, apprehensive Guianese planters had moved to import labourers from elsewhere to be bonded on contracts which were originally fixed at seven years, then lowered to three and finally in 1837 settled at five. They tried a variety of sources for their labour, first of all other West Indian islands, then Britain and Germany, followed by Madeira, China and India, even going to the United States for workers in 1839–40, where they were not successful. The original supplier of labour, the West Coast of Africa, was no longer keen to supply people now that Britain had prohibited the slave trade, and in fact those Africans who did come to B.G. after emancipation—some 14,000—were usually men and women rescued by the Royal Navy from slave ships supplying those New World territories, such as Brazil and Cuba, where slavery was still active.

Very few of these new sources of labour proved satisfactory to the planters. In other West Indian territories there was opposition from the sugar interests at this enticement of their workers, and many of the men themselves looked on work in B.G. as merely temporary, their homes remaining in the islands; from 1835 to 1928 only about 42,500 West Indian contract workers arrived, coming mostly from Barbados and the Windward Islands. The Europeans that were introduced either succumbed to tropical diseases (including rum) or soon migrated from the estates to less arduous and better paid employment in the towns. The Madeiran Portuguese, who although technically white have never been regarded as quite the social equivalent of northern whites by the rest of Guianese society, came chiefly in the 1840s, altogether about 32,000 coming during the whole century. Very soon indeed after their arrival they left the farms and moved strongly into retail trade, by 1851 already owning over 60 per cent of the nearly 800 licensed retail stores. Similarly the Chinese did not stay long on the plantations but moved into other occupations. Partly because there was such a preponderance of men in

the 12,000 who arrived before 1866 (only another 1500 came after that date) the Chinese merged into the society to a very considerable extent. This was in marked contrast with their behaviour in other British sugar territories, especially in Jamaica where until recently they have tended to be socially exclusive, looking backwards to China and maintaining physical contacts with the homeland. This happened very little in B.G.,[10] where there was a substantial amount of miscegenation with all the other races, the process producing some outstandingly beautiful women.

By far the most important immigration in the nineteenth century was that from India. This started in a small way in the 1830s with rather unsuitable labour recruited from Indian cities, but was soon banned by the Indian Government in protest at the terrible conditions of passage and employment. This ban lasted for six years until 1844, and then four years later the British Government made loans available to the West Indies which were in part (and especially in the case of Trinidad and British Guiana) meant to soften the blow of the 1846 Sugar Duties Act, by making it easier to import indentured labour. From then on until 1917 there was a steady stream of officially-sponsored Indian emigration to the sugar lands of the West Indies, which formed part of a broader movement towards sugar that took Indians also to Fiji, Mauritius and Natal. Altogether about 548,000 East Indians came to the British, French and Dutch West Indies on official schemes during this period, about 239,000 to B.G. alone, 134,000 to Trinidad, 78,000 to Guadeloupe and Martinique and 35,000 to Surinam.[11] Of those who came to B.G. about 76,000 returned to India under official auspices and possibly others returned under more private schemes, while

[10] For some of the possible reasons for this, see Morton H. Friede: 'The Chinese in British Guiana', *Social and Economic Studies*, Vol. 5, 1956, especially pp. 69–73.
[11] Augier *et al*. op. cit., p. 210.

large numbers died soon after their arrival, as did so many immigrants.[12]

The new labour was recruited by a system of agents stationed throughout India, and most of the immigrants were from the United Provinces, being mainly agriculturalists of medium-caste status.[13] There was official supervision of the 'amenities' of the passage and on arrival in the colony the immigrants were set to work under a standard contract for five years, working six days a week at one shilling a day for the work, plus free accommodation in old slave quarters or 'coolie lines', and free medical care and hospital accommodation, of which they were frequently in need.[14] After serving out his term the labourer could seek another employer—not necessarily in sugar—or could, until 1854, apply for a free return passage; after that date the terms for paid repatriation became gradually stiffer and stiffer, until after 1898 he himself had to pay half the cost of the return passage even after ten years' stay in B.G.

The Era of the Sugar Bounties

Now that the labour problem was to a large degree solved by the availability of East Indians, sugar production was free to resume the expansion that had marked it before Emancipation. In the eighteen forties and fifties output did not rise above a level of 50,000 tons, but in 1860 it began a period of steady growth that was to take it to around 120,000 tons by 1884. Moreover the price of sugar held up fairly well, in spite of the increasing trend to free trade in the British market; in 1860 the value of the B.G. sugar crop

[12] For example, 'between 1841 and 1851 over 42,300 people entered the colony, but the population increase recorded is only 29,500' (G. W. Roberts: 'Some Observations on the Population of British Guiana', *Population Studies*, Vol. 2, 1948), p. 211.

[13] See Raymond T. Smith: 'Some Characteristics of Indian Immigrants to British Guiana', *Population Studies*, Vol. 13, 1959, pp. 34–49.

[14] It was not until the 1921–1931 decade that census returns for the East Indian population showed an excess of births over deaths, in spite of the high fertility of Indian women.

was about £1.2 million, and in twenty years it had risen to around £2 million.

But just as free trade in sugar was established in Britain in 1874, forces gathered strength that were to turn this liberal ideal into a mockery. In 1855 beet sugar constituted only 10 per cent of world production, but a period of rapid growth fostered by large subsidies in several northern European countries carried the proportion to 40 per cent by 1875, by which time this 'bounty-fed' sugar had begun to make an entrance on the world's export markets. Thereafter its growth on those markets was phenomenal, especially as the method of paying these subsidies was designed—at least in Germany— to increase productivity and so to lower costs, as time went on. In 1874 German sugar exports were negligible, but a decade later they stood at about 650,000 tons. By 1899 almost two thirds of world sugar production was from beet, and prices of raw sugar dropped precipitously from £20 a ton in 1875 to £11¾ a decade later, and to £10 in 1895.[15]

Britain's reaction to this dumping was to maintain a policy of extreme *laissez-faire*. Although West India planters and others vigorously pointed out that true free trade implied the use of countervailing duties against such subsidised exports, there was a steadfast refusal to examine the logic of their case. Free trade meant cheap sugar, and there was a disposition to abandon the West Indies (including B.G.) to the American sphere of influence. Writing in 1876 the Colonial Secretary, Lord Derby, remarked: 'If Germany, Austria and France were taxed to give the British consumer sugar at a cheap price, why complain? The natural market of the West Indies [is] America, not Europe.'[16]

[15] It is interesting to note that the present proportion of beet sugar production is back to almost 40 per cent, while the average world price of raw sugar during 1959–1962 was £23, only a few pounds above the 1875 figure in spite of the enormous fall in the value of money since that time.

[16] Quoted by R. W. Beachey: *The British West Indies Sugar Industry in the Late 19th Century* (Blackwell, Oxford, 1957), p. 55.

And in fact the West Indies did seriously turn their attention to the North American markets, which British Guiana with her relatively modern processing equipment was well placed to supply, compared with some of the older sugar islands. Pressure for some kind of commercial union with North America, and especially with the United States, mounted steadily through the eighties and nineties as subsidised beet sugar took more and more of the British market, and distress in the sugar plantations increased; by 1895 the West Indies supplied only 5 per cent of the U.K. market, compared to 14 per cent ten years before.

By 1896 conditions in the Caribbean were so bad that Joseph Chamberlain, then Colonial Secretary, appointed a Royal Commission to investigate the problem. It found that distress was severe in all the sugar colonies, and was due primarily to the sugar bounties. The Commission could not, however, bring itself to recommend the imposition of countervailing duties, since this would be contrary to 'the settled policy of the United Kingdom'. They added as cold comfort that 'The United States affords the best and the natural market for the West Indies, and if that market should be closed or lost to West Indian sugar the colonies must suffer severely.'[17]

With such Imperial encouragement, B.G. and the islands had been engaged for many years on a series of protracted and frustrating negotiations with various U.S. Administrations; these had been sufficiently successful that by 1900 three-quarters of West Indian sugar exports went to the U.S.A. But these negotiations came to an abrupt end with the Spanish-American War, which was a disaster for the non-Spanish Caribbean. It brought Puerto Rico into the American tariff area and resulted in Cuba and the Philippines being given, by 1903, large preferential margins in the U.S. market. The chief market for West Indian sugar

[17] See *Report of the Royal West India Commission 1897* (Col. 8655), p. 13 and p. 9.

collapsed, disappearing entirely by the end of the first decade of the century.

Luckily the Brussels Convention of 1902 had meanwhile abolished the sugar bounties altogether, but this victory was tempered by the fact that the lowered cost of beet sugar continued to make it competitive even after the subsidies were withdrawn; in 1909, for example, out of a total British sugar import of 1.6 million tons only 129,000 were of cane sugar. A principal support for West Indian sugar at this time was the preference granted unilaterally by Canada in 1898, a preference which may be said to have inaugurated twentieth century 'Imperial Free Trade',[18] and which was certainly a lifeline thrown out at a time of extreme distress. Production of sugar in B.G. did not exceed the 1887 level of 130,000 tons for about half a century, but fluctuated down in the range of 80,000 to 120,000 tons.

It is arguable that it would have been better if the sugar industry in B.G. had died an unnatural death at the hands of the sugar bounties and American discrimination, since she would then have been forced to diversify her agriculture to a considerable degree, and would not now have to depend primarily on a monoculture ruled by only two firms and dependent on special external protection. In neighbouring Surinam the sugar industry did collapse, for it had no substantial Canadian preferences and production conditions were not so favourable; partly as a result, Surinam's agriculture is considerably more diversified, both with respect to commodity and to ownership.

Whatever the merits of this argument—and the collapse of cane-growing in British Guiana would undoubtedly have caused great misery—the facts are that sugar held on through the first thirty-five years of the century, with indeed considerable prosperity in the day of World War I scarcity and high prices, when the value of the crop rose to

[18] See Peter Newman: 'Canada's Role in West Indian Trade before 1912', *Inter American Economic Affairs*, Vol. 14, 1960, pp. 25–49, for an account of this whole period.

around £4 million. Thanks largely to the system of Imperial Preference introduced in the thirties, production rose considerably after 1935, though prices were quite low and the value of the crop was only around £1 million. Production averaged about 190,000 tons in the five years before the war, fell slightly in its last years and then began a rapid climb which took it to its present level of about 330,000 tons. This post-war growth was due first to the British shortage of dollars for buying Cuban sugar, and then to the Commonwealth Sugar Agreement under which B.G. shares with the West Indies a substantial quota on the U.K. market, about two-thirds of which is at a price that is normally substantially above the world price.

It was during the depression of the late eighties and nineties, when the sugar estates' demand for labour was not so pressing, that rice began to assume its importance as a cash crop. Although it had long been grown in a small way by Negroes, rapid progress was not made until Indian sugar estate workers, either at the end of their periods of indenture or during periods of enforced idleness, turned to peasant farming. For them rice was an ideal crop to help establish a farming community, since production conditions were quite favourable, and its cultivation required abilities—and methods of economic and social organisation—that were still remembered from their lives in India.

By 1905 B.G. had attained self-sufficiency in rice and began to export to other countries in the Caribbean area. As with sugar the scarcities of World War I brought prosperity and by 1917 rice exports were at the respectable level of £300,000. Accompanying this trend to a firmly established cash agriculture, the East Indian community shifted from living mainly on the sugar estates to a much more evenly balanced distribution. In 1890 only about 30 per cent of the Indians lived off the estates, while by 1911 more than half of them did so; and with the ending of indentured immigration during the 1914–1918 war, this

change in the character of the East Indian community continued.

In this way the present pattern of the community became established. In the country there was a large resident population on the sugar estates, principally of East Indians but including Negroes as well, and close to the estates were villages—often containing both races living side by side—which supplied part-time and seasonal labour to the plantations and sugar mills. There were also communities of Indian rice farmers, especially in Berbice and West Demerara, which had little to do with the sugar economy and which tended therefore to be isolated from the rest of the society, though not wholly so. In the towns the Negroes, 'Mixed', Chinese and Whites predominated, while in the interior there were Amerindians and the enclaves of the mining camps, staffed mainly by Negroes. The most important of these enclaves were those of the bauxite companies, the first of which was started during the first World War.

These three products of sugar, rice and bauxite dominate the economy, and the methods of economic organisation used to produce the first two dominate the society as well.

III. DEMOGRAPHIC AND SOCIAL PRESSURES

In addition to forces rooted in its history and its physical environment, present-day British Guiana is subject to pressures that have their origin in the rapid acceleration of population growth, and in the pattern of social development that has established itself. This chapter discusses these determinants of change, paying particular attention to the demographic factor, on which only recently has detailed data for the post-war period become available. The treatment of social structure and dynamics is more cursory than would have been necessary if the classic account contained in Chapter V of Raymond Smith's *British Guiana* had not been available.

1. *Population Growth: The General Pattern*

Since the time of Malthus social scientists have been keenly aware of the close interaction between economic development and population growth, and more recently have become increasingly conscious that many other factors besides those dealt with by economics enter into the determination of the growth of population. Social attitudes to the size of families, the level of the education provided for women in the society, knowledge of good nutritional practices, all these and many more non-economic forces help to shape the evolution of population structure, and it is a difficult matter indeed to disentangle the role that each plays. Perhaps the most important development in recent decades, especially in the tropics, has been the enormous improvement in the standard of public health services, both through the general provision of medical care and sanitation, and in the more specific field of the prevention of infectious diseases, as with the eradication of malaria.

It is impossible to discuss demographic problems seriously
without a fairly detailed quantitative basis, which is
provided in Table 1. This table gives a summary picture of
demographic development in B.G. over the last generation,
and is perhaps best approached by first noting column (7),
which shows how greatly the death rate has fallen over this
period. There was a steady but slow decline in this before
1945, followed by a much more rapid fall thereafter, to a
level that is now less than half that of thirty years ago.
Similarly from column (6), we can see that from an earlier
level around thirty-three per thousand the birth rate has
climbed into the lower forties, which together with move-
ments in the death rate has produced a major upsurge in
the rate of natural increase. From column (9), there was a
clear growth in this rate during the first half of the period,
but this was fairly slow until it exploded into the great
acceleration of the post-war period; in 1957–1961 the
average rate of increase was at the remarkable level of 33.5
per thousand, fully three times the rate of twenty years
before.

The actual numbers represented by this upsurge are
shown in columns (2) to (4) and—graphically and in more
detail—in the diagram on page 36, which is based on the
annual data from which Table 1 was calculated.

In the early period the net additions to the Guianese
population were only of the order of 3000–5000 a year on
average, supplemented (except during the war) by a small
amount of immigration. After the war this annual increase
more than tripled, though its effect was very slightly
reduced by emigration that was on a scale much smaller
than that from Jamaica. It is quite remarkable that even
though the population in 1961 was more than half as large
again as that of 1946, for no year in the intervening period
did the number of deaths climb above 6000 nor sink below
5000, while at the same time the annual number of
births rose by over 10,000 from 13,061 in 1946 to 23,797
in 1961.

Table 1. Vital Statistics for British Guiana, 1931-1961

Period	Col. (1) Population at end of year	Col. (2) Number of registered live births	Col. (3) Number of registered deaths	Col. (4) Natural increase of population	Col. (5) Net immigration (+) or emigration (−)	Col. (6) Crude birth rate per 1000 population	Col. (7) Crude death rate per 1000 population	Col. (8) Rate of natural increase per 1000	Col. (9) Infant mortality rate per 1000 live births
Average 1931–1935	320,816	10,340	7226	3114	+509	32·2	22·5	9·7	141
,, 1936–1940	339,135	10,922	7199	3723	+30	32·2	21·2	11·0	119
,, 1941–1945	364,294	12,525	7087	5438	−115	34·4	19·4	15·0	112
,, 1946–1951	395,018	15,835	5560	10,275	+13	40·5	14·3	26·2	81
,, 1952–1956	460,692	19,737	5644	14,113	−1140	43·5	12·5	31·0	75
,, 1957–1961	535,438	23,056	5297	17,759	−1857	43·5	10·0	33·5	60

Note: Data for 1931–45 includes the registered Amerindian population (about 8000–16,000 during this period), while post-war data do not.

Sources: 1931–45: R. R. Kuczynski: *A Demographic Survey of the British Colonial Empire, Volume II* (London, Oxford University Press for the Royal Institute of International Affairs, 1953), Chapter XXI, Tables on pp. 151 and 178.

1946–58: *Annual Report of the Registrar General, 1958* (Georgetown, Government Printer, 1962), Tables 2, 23 and 25.

1959–61: Columns (2) to (4) from *Quarterly Statistical Digest, September 1962* (Georgetown, Government Printer, 1963), Tables 6 and 7. Columns (5) to (9) from *United Nations Demographic Year-book 1962* (New York, 1963), Tables 25, 26, 14, 18 and 17. Column (1)—calculated from Columns (2), (3) and (5). All figures for 1960 and 1961 are provisional.

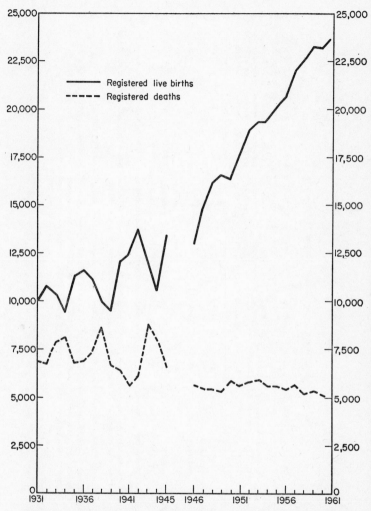

The data for 1931–45 unfortunately include unreliable figures for the registered Amerindian population (about 8000 to 16,000 during this period), while the post-war data do not.

The causes of this rapid acceleration have not yet been analysed in detail, although several writers have given the credit (or laid the blame, according to point of view) to the very effective D.D.T. campaign carried out in 1945–47 against malaria, which resulted in its almost complete eradication on the coastal plains. Conditions in the coastal waterways of B.G. were in fact ideal for the propagation of this disease. To quote the malariologist who was mainly responsible for the campaign:

In this Colony, perhaps more than elsewhere, the connection between agriculture and malaria is intimate; there can be no doubt that the prevailing forms of cultivation, rice and sugar cane, influence the malaria problem adversely . . . Thus ideally favourable breeding sites are provided for mosquitoes, at all seasons, and breeding continues the year around with greater or lesser intensity, according to the temperature and the individual characteristics of each species.[1]

Moreover the fluctuations in births and in deaths that were so noticeable before and during the war, and which show up clearly in the diagram, can be correlated closely with the existence of malarial epidemics on the coast. There were serious outbreaks in 1938 and again in 1943–44, and the effects of these manifested themselves both in high death rates in those years and in low birth rates a year later, since malaria lowers the rate of conception and increases the tendency to abort. In 1940–42 there were severe drought conditions on the coast, especially in 1941, and the resultant use of seawater in many of the canals greatly affected the population of *anopheles darlingii*, which was the chief vector of malaria. As a result the disease all but disappeared over large areas, resulting in remarkably favourable vital rates, for in 1941 the death rate was only 15·6 (compare 15·5 for 1946) and in 1942 the

[1] G. Giglioli: 'Malaria in British Guiana: Part I', *Agricultural Journal of British Guiana*, Vol. 9, 1938, pp. 75–81.

birth rate was as high as 38·2 (compared with 39·9 for 1947).[2]

However, before ascribing the population upsurge entirely to malaria eradication, it should be borne in mind that already in the earlier period there were significant increases in the rate of natural growth (see column 8) which, if continued, would in any case have resulted in rates of increase of around twenty per thousand or more in the post-war period. In addition the considerable rise in income *per capita* experienced after the war would have tended to improve vital rates considerably. A recent and detailed study by the author has in fact estimated that in B.G. about forty per cent of the rise in population growth that occurred should be attributed to the anti-malaria campaign, the balance presumably being due to other forces of the kind described.[3]

As we have often emphasised, British Guiana has for all of its history felt itself to be deficient in numbers of people. As late as 1948, the West Indian demographer G. W. Roberts could write that 'for British Guiana, so short of population, the problem is how to prolong this lag [between falling mortality and falling fertility] in order to secure the maximum expansion'.[4] And there is certainly a very real sense in which British Guiana *is* extremely under-populated, for it only has about seven people per square mile of the whole area. The real question however—given the way in which B.G. has developed—is whether the coastal sugar 'island' is now over-populated. This is a difficult problem to answer, partly because much of the development that has taken place until recently has not been based on a situation

---

[2] The rates for 1941 and 1942 have led some writers to argue, erroneously, that malaria eradication had little to do with the population explosion, since rates characteristic of the post-war period had already been achieved by those years.

[3] Peter Newman: *Malaria Eradication and Population Growth*, a monograph to be published in 1964 by the School of Public Health, University of Michigan.

[4] G. W. Roberts, op. cit., p. 215.

of high labour supply relative to needs, but instead has been influenced by past patterns of labour scarcity. It is indeed probable that by efficient re-organisation and vigorous planning the existing coastal strip could absorb most of the labour likely to be available during the next decade or so. But what is certain is that the sudden onrush of population has had a disorganising effect, on a society and economy that until recently was geared to the opposite situation.

The Age Distribution of the Population

One of the characteristics of greatly accelerated population growth is that it often changes the age structure of the population in a definite pattern, shifting the 'centre of gravity' of the distribution towards the younger age groups. This shift is brought about mainly by the rise in fertility that occurs, though the falling death rate—which often affects infants more than any other group—plays a minor role as well.

These changes are shown for B.G. in Tables 2a and 2b, which demonstrate clearly how over time the population has become markedly younger. In 1921 less than one third of the population was under 15, while in 1960 almost one half of the population was below that age. The magnitude of the shift is dramatically illustrated by the last line of Table 2b, which shows the average number of dependents that each person of working age (i.e. those between 15 and 64) had to support.[5] In 1921 there were almost twice as many people of working age as there were in all other age groups, so that the average number of dependents was just over one half. By 1946 the age distribution had changed sufficiently to increase this ratio to three quarters, while by 1960 each person of working age had to support one full dependent.

[5] Throughout this section the argument assumes for the sake of simplicity that each person of working age is actually in the labour force, though of course many are not, especially among married women.

TABLE 2a. *Age Distribution of the Population, 1921–1960*

Age Group	1921 Census	1931 Census	1946 Census	1960 Census
Over 0 and under 5	30,754	45,077	62,732	98,195
,, 5 ,, ,, 15	64,613	66,369	84,338	161,075
,, 15 ,, ,, 45	148,448	146,563	162,241	215,255
,, 45 ,, ,, 64	42,666	43,607	47,597	67,072
Over 65	9136	8459	12,422	18,809
Age not stated	2074	858	348	—
Total	297,691	310,933	369,678	560,406

TABLE 2b. *Percentage Distribution of Table 2a, for those whose Age was Stated*

Over 0 and under 5	10·4	14·5	17·0	17·5
,, 5 ,, ,, 15	21·9	21·4	22·8	28·7
,, 15 ,, ,, 45	50·2	47·3	43·9	38·4
,, 45 ,, ,, 64	14·4	14·1	12·9	12·0
Over 65	3·1	2·7	3·4	3·4
Total	100·0	100·0	100·0	100·0

	1921	1931	1946	1960
Number of dependents per person of working age (15 to 64)	0·55	0·63	0·76	0·98

Sources: 1921 and 1931, R. R. Kuczynski, op. cit., Table on p. 158
1964, R. R. Kuczynski, op. cit., Table 4, p. 160
1960, Census Bulletins No. 1 and No. 12, *Population Census 1960, Series D, British Guiana* (Port of Spain, Population Census Division, 1963).

The significance of this is that the productivity per person in the labour force has had to rise substantially (by about one third) over this period simply in order to maintain *per capita* incomes constant, let alone to increase them, since an increasingly smaller proportion of the population is actually of working age. An average worker's income of $300 in 1921 would have meant a national average then of $200, while today the corresponding figure would be only $150. It is important to bear in mind, therefore, that a large part of each increase in real income that has occurred has been siphoned off into maintaining an ever-larger proportion of the population out of the labour force,

especially since the war. An obvious burden paid for out of this is the considerably increased cost of education that occurs when the school age population almost doubles, as it did from 1946–1960. A further problem is the possibility of severe juvenile unemployment when the crest of this wave of increased births reaches working age, as must now be happening since it is seventeen years since the sustained high birth rates began.

Differences in Rates of Growth by Race

Throughout this century there have been marked differences in the rates of growth in the numbers of the various races living in British Guiana. We have already seen that it was not until the 1921–1931 decade that the natural increase of the East Indian population became a positive magnitude, but after that time the increasing numbers of women in that population, and their increasing fertility as incomes rose, pushed up the Indian birth rate more than sufficiently to compensate for the higher death rates on the malaria-ridden sugar estates and paddy lands. As time went on, and especially after the war, the generally low death rates and their extraordinarily high fertility rates raised the rate of natural increase of the East Indians well above that of the others.

TABLE 3. Inter-Censal Annual Rates of Increase, by Race, 1911–1960
(per cent per year)

Period	East Indians	Negroes	Mixed	All other races excluding Amerindians	Total Colony excluding Amerindians
1911–21	−0·4	+0·1	+0·1	−0·6	+0·0
1921–31	+0·4	+0·6	+1·0	−1·3	+0·5
1931–46	+1·4	+1·0	+0·8	+0·4	+1·1
1946–60	+3·6	+1·9	+4·2	+0·5	+2·9

Sources: See Sources for Tables 4a and 4b.

Table 3 shows quite clearly the much more rapid rate of growth in the numbers of East Indians than of Negroes in the post-war period. It is probable however that some of the

Negro increase has in fact been absorbed into the 'Mixed' category. In a society where there has been as much miscegenation as there has in B.G., the self-designation 'Mixed' told to the census-taker is more an articulation of a state of mind, probably indicative of social aspirations in a colonial society, than it is a clear and separate category. Much of the very rapid post-war growth in this heterogeneous group must certainly be due to such socially motivated 'switching'; but even allowing for this factor, the East Indian growth rate is still well above that of the Negroes.

The effect of these differing rates of growth on the racial composition of the population is shown in Tables 4a and 4b. A curious feature of the Census returns has been the separation of 'Portuguese' from 'Other Europeans', a separation which reflected the special status of the Portuguese in the society and had of course nothing to do with differing racial origins. As the declining population of these Portuguese is probably accounted for by mixing with other groups, rather than by migration, the distinction has become increasingly less tenable, and in the 1960 Census was dropped altogether.

The salient feature of this Table is the increasing proportion of East Indians, especially after the second World War, so that by 1960 they constituted half of the non-Amerindian population.[6] Since much of this increase took place fairly recently, it is probable that East Indians do not yet constitute a majority of the population that is eligible to vote, although it is only a matter of time before this happens, especially if the voting age is put down to eighteen, as Dr. Jagan wishes.

The Geographical Distribution of the Population

Another peculiarity of British Guiana, as we have seen, is not only that the East Indian population is growing

[6] The rapid growth of the Amerindian population is due mainly to improvements in Census-taking in the interior, except possibly for the 1946–1960 increase.

TABLE 4a. Census Returns by Race, 1911–1960

Census Year	East Indians	Negroes	Mixed	Chinese	Portuguese	Other Europeans	All other races except Amerindian	Total colony excluding Amerindian	Amerindian
1911	126,517	115,846	30,251	2623	10,084	3937	243	289,140	6901
1921	124,938	117,169	30,587	2722	9175	3291	659	288,540	9150
1931	130,540	124,203	33,800	2951	8612	2127	352	302,585	8348
1946	163,434	143,385	37,685	3567	8543	2480	285	359,379	16,322
1960	267,840	183,980	67,189	4074	11,873			534,956	25,450

TABLE 4b. Percentage Composition of the Population by Race, 1911–1960

Census Year	Total non-Amerindian population	East Indians	Negroes	Mixed	All others except Amerindians
1911	289,140	43·8	39·9	10·5	5·8
1921	288,540	43·3	40·6	10·6	5·5
1931	302,585	43·1	41·0	11·2	4·7
1946	359,379	45·5	39·9	10·5	4·1
1960	534,956	50·1	34·4	12·6	3·0

Sources: 1911–1931, G. W. Roberts, op. cit., Table 1, p. 186
1946, R. R. Kuczynski, op. cit., Table 1, p. 153
1960, Census Bulletin No. 1, Population Census 1960, Series D, British Guiana (Port of Spain, Population Census Division, 1963).

faster than the rest, but that it is also much more rural in its geographical distribution. Only about 29 per cent of the population was urban in 1960, and of this group only 22 per cent were East Indian, the great majority (70 per cent) being Negro or Mixed; these figures are implicit in Tables 5a and 5b. It will be noticed that the Negro-Mixed concentrations in the towns are balanced by similar concentrations of East Indians in West Demerara and Berbice, while Essequibo has a very large percentage of the Amerindians.

This rather marked difference in the geographical distribution of the population by race has had an important effect on the society and its politics, in that there has been a natural barrier to the intermingling of East Indians with other races, except in the more urban middle classes. This is not to say that there have been no contacts, but they have not been so numerous as would have been desirable for a fully integrated society. The three main industries of sugar, rice and bauxite have little inter-connection, and so the two cultures—East Indian and Negro-Mixed—have tended to separate out under the impact of the technologies used by these main primary producers. Not the least of the benefits of a vigorous development programme, with a focus on the opening-up of the interior, would be its role in knitting together the urban and rural sectors in a major effort that would need the full co-operation of both in order to be successful.

Social Structure and Dynamics

In order to discuss the present pattern of social development it is necessary to begin with the original pattern in B.G., which was that of the slave plantations. One has to ponder how it was that a small number of whites and near-whites could control a much greater Negro population, and more importantly how they secured the day-to-day acquiescence of the slaves in work that was always arduous and often exhausting. It is true that discipline was normally

TABLE 5a. Geographical Distribution of the Population, by Race, 1960

Region	East Indians	Negroes	Mixed	All other except Amerindians	Amerindian	Total including Amerindians
British Guiana	267,840	183,980	67,189	15,947	25,450	560,406
Urban						
Georgetown and suburbs	32,474	72,027	32,769	10,729	403	148,402
New Amsterdam	3476	7580	2523	445	35	14,059
Rural						
East Demerara	68,351	45,179	10,122	2318	1434	127,404
West Demerara	42,848	15,646	2920	709	96	62,219
Berbice	91,470	27,350	6918	657	1599	127,994
Essequibo	29,221	16,198	11,937	1089	21,883	80,328

TABLE 5b. Percentage Distribution of Table 5a

Region	East Indians	Negroes	Mixed	All other except Amerindians	Amerindian	Total including Amerindians
British Guiana	47·8	32·8	12·0	2·8	4·5	100·0
Urban						
Georgetown and suburbs	21·9	48·5	22·1	7·2	0·3	100·0
New Amsterdam	24·7	53·9	17·9	3·2	0·2	100·0
Rural						
East Demerara	53·6	35·5	7·9	1·8	1·1	100·0
West Demerara	68·9	25·1	4·7	1·1	0·2	100·0
Berbice	71·5	21·4	5·4	0·5	1·2	100·0
Essequibo	36·4	20·2	14·9	1·4	27·2	100·0

Source: Census Bulletin No. 1, referred to in Tables 2 and 4.

severe, that there were in fact several major slave uprisings
and that there existed a militia of whites and free 'coloureds'
to help put down such revolts, often with chilling barbarity.
But oppressive physical compulsion alone, given the small
number of oppressors, cannot explain the immense amount
of labour that was invested in the creation of the plantations,
especially of the sugar estates on the coast, with their
elaborate systems of drainage and irrigation trenches.

The solution to this problem seems to lie in the social
system evolved by the estates, which won at least a passive
acceptance among most of the slaves. At the top, the
hierarchy consisted of the owners, or more usually managers
acting for absentee owners in Britain—the latter consisting
of such people as Sir Thomas Bertram of Mansfield Park.
In the middle ranks of overseers and artisans there were
poorer whites, as well as the free 'men of colour', the
offspring of richer Europeans and Negro slave women, who
were often set free by their fathers and indeed well educated
by them, sometimes in Europe. At the bottom were the
slaves, who were themselves divided into hierarchies, with
the locally born ranked above those from Africa, and
'house slaves' above the 'field slaves'.

The whole complex system was cemented together by a
high valuation of European—and especially English—
culture, and a corresponding denigration of all things
African. The very aloofness of the top ranks among the
English made the system easier to enforce, since most of
these were essentially birds of passage in the country,
looking towards 'home' and going there to die, if the
tropics did not get them first; this focus of the *élite* on the
far-off culture of England naturally helped in its elevation
to the status of an unattainable ideal. Further, the
detribalisation that was an inevitable accompaniment of
slave getting and transporting, and of the crowded conditions on the plantations, made it necessary for many of the
uprooted Africans to preserve their psychological equili-
brium by identifying with a new culture; and the social

system of the estates lay ready to hand, even though in it they were assigned to the lowest place.

Because English was 'white' and African was 'black', the form in which these cultural values manifested themselves in the society was as a preference scale based on colour, with African black at the bottom and ranging up through local 'black, brown and beige' to the near-whites and thence to the whites at the top. But this colour scale was only an *index* to the value scale, and was not the value scale itself. Once slavery was ended it was quite possible for a black man, gravely handicapped though he admittedly was by his colour, to ascend the social ladder if he showed exceptional aptitude for things European, especially in absorbing a European education and outlook. Once some way up he could take a lighter-skinned wife, and the children he would have by her would then start off from their father's higher position, unless one of them were so unfortunate as to be both black *and* slow-witted, in which case he would probably descend by the way his father had come.

As the original offspring of black-white unions themselves intermarried through several generations, the spectrum between the two colours became completely filled in with all possible shades, and social distinctions became correspondingly finer drawn. But it must be emphasised that the basic criterion was conformity to the European cultural pattern, and that the test of colour, although very important, was in essence secondary to the test of performance, so much so that several full Negroes in high positions were (and are) classed as 'white' within Guianese society. This pattern, which was similar to those of most of the other sugar islands, was in marked contrast with that of the United States, where even the slightest tinge of colour constituted an absolute barrier, regardless of ability, unless one could 'pass' into the white population as one of themselves; and it was in some contrast also with the patterns in Latin America, where the test of colour was generally less stringent.

The Impact of Immigration

It is convenient to use the term 'creole society' to denote the social system that we have been describing, a system based on the sugar economy and embracing the White, Mixed and Negro groups. Although in many ways— especially in its snobbery of class and colour—not an entirely attractive society, it did have the merit of being fairly stable, and it survived the period of emancipation with little change, except of course in the legal status of the majority of its members. As we have seen, the conditions of agriculture on the coast ensured that most of the Negroes would remain dependent for their cash incomes in part at least on the plantation economy, and this meant that they remained part of creole society. Upward mobility for the darker-skinned Negroes naturally increased, especially by the avenue of education opened by the increasing number of Christian missionaries. As time went on these Negroes moved into school-teaching, the professions and the civil services, although of course the top posts in these continued to be held by whites and lightly coloured men.

The streams of new immigrants that followed on emancipation at first posed few problems for creole society. The new Africans and the West Indians were easily absorbed, and so were the Madeiran Portuguese and the Chinese, partly because there were relatively few of either of these groups, and partly because their light skins placed them almost immediately high up in the hierarchy, though not necessarily—as we have noted—quite on a par with Europeans 'proper'.

The East Indians set a quite different problem, however, especially as their numbers grew to significant proportions. On the one hand their usually brown colour would have earned them a middle-ranking place in creole society, but on the other their quite different customs and religions, their poverty and their consequent willingness to accept miserable slave-like conditions on the estates, led to the

semi-official designation of them as 'coolies' becoming often a term of scorn among the creoles. For their part, the Indians at first concentrated on survival in alien and difficult surroundings, and then, as they became established, turned to the task of climbing out of their poverty, especially as they ended their periods of indenture and tended to move into rice cultivation.

The crowded conditions in the coolie lines, in which people with widely differing backgrounds were jumbled together, plus the general shortage of Indian women, meant that the minimal conditions of social organisation required for the careful observance of Indian religious ritual and of the caste system were just not feasible on the estates, and as a result caste, religion and language became greatly attenuated as governing forces among the East Indians. Even so, however, what customs did survive among them were markedly different from those of the 'ideal' creole culture, while their comparative geographical isolation on the estates cut them off from the influence of the centres of creole society, such as Georgetown, at a time when the means of mass communication were much less developed than now.

Thus the Indians tended to develop the traits character-istic of poor minority immigrants in most places in the world, working hard and saving hard in their efforts to gain a firm place in the community. In this way a myth grew up among the creole population, especially in the towns, about the allegedly fierce economic drives and extreme thriftiness of the Indians. This probably had a flimsy basis in the first place, but now has little or no validity, at least as regards thrift. Surveys of household budgets show that Indians spend just as much—if not more —on the good things of life such as clothes and alcohol as does the rest of the population.

As the Indian minority grew larger and began to free itself more and more from dependence on the sugar estates, the problem of fitting into creole society became

more acute, especially in the middle classes and in the towns. In the country the estate-oriented communities of Indians and Negroes lived in genuinely peaceful co-existence, while the poorer Indian rice farmers, though more isolated, were still in broad harmony with the other rural people. But in the urban bourgeoisie especially, and even among the rural middle-class, the creole society tended to reject their Indian counterparts, except for a few Indian professional men and merchants who deliberately shed all traces of 'coolie' behaviour. For the rest, their difficulty with the English language and their different modes of life, plus their potential threat to creole jobs and influence, were enough to prevent acceptance. Not unnaturally, this rebuff produced a counter-reaction among the Indians, which led them to stress the value of traditional Indian ways of life in the Guianese context. But this should not be seen as an actual resurgence of Indian culture but rather, as Smith has pointed out, as 'a mode of expression of [their] desire to be treated on terms of equality within a Guianese universe. It is most emphatically not an expression of separatist tendencies.'[7]

At this point it might be worth drawing attention to two aspects of what could be termed the 'mathematical sociology' of the Guianese situation, each of which I would judge operates to increase the tensions that exist, though I could easily be wrong. The first arises from the fact that the immigration process has, by historical accident, resulted in only one major new population in B.G., and thus tension is between only two groups and tends to get polarised rather than negotiated, particularly as the power of the imperialist 'umpire' fades away, and the prospects of independence loom ahead. This may be contrasted with the situation in Surinam, where indentured immigration supplied not only a population of East Indians, but also a sizeable group of Javanese, in addition to the creoles imported under slavery.

[7] Raymond Smith, op. cit., p. 111.

Since these Javanese can tip the balance in favour of whichever side they choose, tensions can be resolved by three-cornered negotiation, rather than ending in direct confrontation. This compromise may make for weak government, but at least it prevents explosion.

The second aspect—and this is even more tentative in direction than the first—is the curiously 'linear' structure of the Guianese population. Strung out in a long line along the coast as they are, it is probably true that there tends to be less communication between the various settlements than there would be if they occupied a more compact rectangular or circular area; and this may result in there being less scope for knowledge of each other's customs than would otherwise have been the case; some research on these topics might prove very interesting.

Modern Developments

To return now to the creole society, this has undergone significant modifications in the last century. Perhaps the most important trend has been that in the consolidation of the sugar estates, so that now only two companies are left in control, each operating on a very large scale. This has had several implications. First, it has entailed the disappearance of a class of creole landowners, and has therefore thrown the focus of leadership of the creole middle-classes to the professional men and merchants of the towns, apart from a few school-teachers and such in the country. This in turn has reduced their leadership's knowledge of and interest in rural affairs, and tended to exaggerate the importance which they place on urban conditions and reactions, especially in Georgetown.

Secondly, the increased 'industrialisation' of the sugar estates brought about by large-scale mechanisation has created a body of workers analogous rather to an industrial proletariat than to agricultural labourers in the British sense of that term. The very size of these sugar companies— and the same goes for the mining concerns—has meant

that they are so large relative to the society which contains them that an individual Guianese can feel little identification with the economic life of his country, whereas he could more easily do so on an early nineteenth century estate. It is therefore not surprising that there has been a strong left-wing movement among estate workers and some of the urban proletariat, both Indian and Negro, and that until fairly recently this common political aim has swamped the racial difference between them.[8] Nor is it surprising that many of the urban creole bourgeoisie feared this left-wing drive of the creole estate and urban workers, and have—again until recently—maintained a gulf between them and these 'Reds'. Given past history, it is only to be expected that the more conservative elements in the towns have been mainly the light-skinned middle-classes, including especially the Portuguese and several of the richer Indian professional men and merchants. It is the darker-skinned Negro middle-class, including especially the intelligentsia and those in the civil service, who have been in sympathy with and indeed have led the left-wing creole workers. It is only in the last few years that this gap between the classes has tended to close, under pressure—real and imagined—from the Indians.

The latter community, with its much faster rate of growth, has increasingly moved into the professions and the civil service as its level of education has improved, and has now gone some way towards taking up the proportion of such jobs that its size would lead one to expect. Naturally this movement has increased the fears of the creole middle-class (of both political persuasions) and so has led to increased tensions. But I would completely agree with Smith in his emphasis on the strong forces at work making for increased 'creolisation' of the Indians; many of us outside observers have greatly underrated this tendency, and sometimes—as in the case of the Robertson Constitutional

---

[8] We leave until Chapter V a discussion of the causes and consequences of the recent racial split among these workers.

Commission of 1954—have ignored it altogether. Patterns of social behaviour have moved towards coincidence in the two communities, especially among the younger people, and there is an underlying feeling that race should not be an important factor in determining personal status in the society.

However this tendency to creolisation is not the only force at work. In the next two chapters we shall see how insufficient economic progress, ineffective political leadership on both sides, and unimaginative and ungenerous handling of the situation by the imperial power have enabled the divisive forces in the society to take hold in recent years, and so to bring the country's social progress to a standstill.

RECENT PERFORMANCE

IV. THE PERFORMANCE OF THE ECONOMY SINCE 1953

IN Part II we concentrate on the behaviour of the economy and developments in Guianese political life since 1953, a year which marked a political turning-point of major significance. In April 1953 elections were held under a new constitution which granted a substantial measure of self-government. Six months later the constitution was suspended and almost direct colonial rule put in its place, on the grounds that the irresponsible behaviour of the elected ministers made the constitution unworkable and threatened 'Communist subversion'. Most of the developments in politics since then can be traced from that traumatic experience, its causes and its consequences.

As far as the economy is concerned, we may divide this period into two distinct parts, the first up to and including 1960, for which rather plentiful data are available; and the second the years from 1961 on, for which there is very little information indeed, the administrative machine having fallen seriously behind in gathering and making available the necessary statistics on which a careful analysis must be based.

1. *The Period 1953–1960: General Trends*

As in the case of demographic changes, economic developments cannot be discussed sensibly without a detailed quantitative background, which is provided in Table 6.

TABLE 6. *Basic Economic Statistics for British Guiana, 1953–1960*
(millions of West Indian dollars unless otherwise stated)

	1953	1954	1955	1956	1957	1958	1959	1960
1. Personal consumption expenditure	136·1	143·7	146·2	158·5	167·4	172·1	178·2	191·8
2. Government current expenditure	21·8	22·2	26·0	28·4	32·2	32·8	33·5	35·8
3. Gross capital formation, public and private	24·5	38·4	46·0	48·0	62·6	68·5	56·9	85·4
4. Exports of goods and services	85·5	87·9	93·1	98·2	114·6	104·0	110·8	134·8
5. Imports of goods and services	72·8	80·9	95·4	100·9	120·9	119·2	113·7	149·8
6. Net indirect taxes	19·2	19·7	24·3	25·4	24·3	24·2	26·3	28·2
7. Gross domestic product at factor cost	175·8	191·7	191·5	206·9	231·6	234·1	239·4	269·9
8. Net income payments to rest of the world	10·3	9·9	9·4	11·1	14·6	11·2	11·4	13·8
9. Depreciation allowances	7·6	7·8	8·9	8·4	15·4	15·4	15·6	17·7
10. National income	157·9	174·0	173·2	187·4	201·5	207·5	212·4	238·3
11. Household net income	150·4	165·6	160·5	175·0	181·5	184·4	189·0	213·7
12. Cost of living index (1959=100)	89·9	92·6	95·3	97·0	98·4	98·3	100·0	100·3
13. Population at mid-year including Amerindians ('000)	459·0	472·2	486·0	500·2	515·5	532·1	549·9	566·8
14. *Per capita* household net income at constant 1959 prices ($)	364	379	347	361	358	353	344	376
15. Terms of trade (1956=100)	102	102	98	100	112	106	111	108
16. Exports as a percentage of national income (%)	54·1	50·5	53·8	52·4	56·9	50·1	52·2	56·6

Notes: (a) Row 7 is obtained as follows: 7 = 1 + 2 + 3 + 4 − 5 − 6.
(b) Row 10 is obtained as follows: 10 = 7 − 8 − 9.
(c) Row 14 is obtained as follows: 14 = 11 ÷ (12 × 13).
In each case sums of individual items may not add to total because of rounding off to one decimal point only.

Sources: (i) Rows 1–10; Table 2–1 in A. Kundu: 'The Economy of British Guiana, 1960–1975', *Social and Economic Studies*, Vol. 12, September 1963, pp. 307–380; this Table was itself based on previous work by Percival, D'Andrade, O'Loughlin and Kundu himself; for references see Kundu's article.
(ii) Rows 11–13; A. Kundu, op. cit., Table 2–3. Kundu's population figures refer to end of year, and have been interpolated here to obtain mid-year estimates.
(iii) Row 14; See Notes in this Table.
(iv) Row 15; *Quarterly Statistical Digest*, March 1962 (Statistical Bureau, Georgetown), Table 33.
(v) Row 16; Row 4 divided by Row 10, multiplied by 100.

Row 10 shows the value of the national income, which increased by 51 per cent during this period. But this does not allow for the falling value of money—prices rose by about 12 per cent—nor for the increasing population, a rise of 23.5 per cent. Hence real incomes *per capita* did not rise by nearly so much, and indeed Row 14 shows that household net income *per capita* (which is defined as personal consumption plus personal savings) hardly rose at all in real terms during this period. The average real income for 1953–56 was $363 and that for 1957–60 was $358, a difference which is not statistically significant.

Therefore we can say that from 1953 to 1960 the economy grew just about fast enough, on average, to maintain real incomes intact. And these incomes were not low by the standards of the underdeveloped world, for an annual household income of 360 BWI dollars is £75, and that is about three times the level of incomes in much of Africa and many of the countries of Asia; nor is it low by Latin American standards. But compared with the recent performance of the Jamaican and Trinidadian economies, the B.G. real growth rate of about 3 per cent was sorely disappointing. In 1953 the Jamaican and B.G. national incomes *per capita* were about the same, and that of Trinidad was perhaps as much as 20 per cent higher. But in Jamaica the gross domestic product at factor cost (GDP) grew in constant price terms at almost 9 per cent per year from 1953 to 1959, while in Trinidad the corresponding figure was even higher, at nearly 11 per cent; hence by 1959 Jamaican national income *per capita* was about £115 and in Trinidad around £160, both a long way from the corresponding Guianese figure of £80.[1]

[1] These figures for the two islands are derived from statistics contained in articles by Carleen O'Loughlin and Eric Armstrong, on Jamaica and Trinidad respectively, to be found in *Social and Economic Studies*, Vol. 12, September 1963.

It should be observed that national income *per capita* and household net income *per capita* are slightly different concepts. In B.G. the former was $386 in 1959, compared to $344 for the latter or £80 compared to £72.

Moreover some of Guiana's growth may be attributed, as Row 15 shows, not to the increases of production but to faster growth in her export prices than her import prices, so that the terms of trade turned in her favour. This was in marked contrast with the experience of most of the under-developed world during this period, where the terms of trade deteriorated considerably; for example those of Uganda fell by about 35 per cent. This difference is due mainly to the role played by the Commonwealth Sugar Agreement in B.G., and to the fictitious nature of the 'price' paid for her bauxite exports. These latter are mainly intra-company transactions of Aluminium Company of Canada Ltd. and of Reynolds Metals, and hence are subject neither to market valuations nor fluctuations.

Before leaving Table 6 we should point to some of its other interesting aspects. Row 2 shows Government's current expenditure, but does not include its expenditure on development projects, which is concealed in Row 3; only a part of Government *revenue* is shown (Row 6) but in fact total revenue during this period was fairly steady at about 23 per cent of national income, which is quite a high proportion for a poor country, although not unbearable. Row 3 shows that total capital information (including investment in stocks) fluctuated enormously over this period, from a low point of about 14 per cent of GDP (gross domestic product) in 1953 to almost 32 per cent in 1960, the latter figure representing a remarkable rate of investment. Indeed the rise in capital formation of $28.5 million from 1959 to 1960 almost alone accounts for the rise in GDP of $30.5 million between those years. This rise in capital was due mainly to heavy investments in manganese mining, in an alumina plant (costing $65 million in total), and in the sugar industry in that year, and not to increases in the Government's development expenditure.

Finally, let us note from the Table the economy's very heavy dependence on exports (Row 16), and the

rather large payments abroad in profits and interest (Row 8.) Exports were consistently over half of the national income, and there was no tendency for this proportion to decrease; rather it increased, from a 1953-56 average of 52.7 per cent to a 1957-60 average of 54.0 per cent. The factor payments abroad indicate that for many activities, especially in mining and to a lesser extent in sugar, much of the earnings accrued is repatriated and so does not get into the domestic income stream. This is also true for the interest on public debt, much of which goes overseas, and which rose from an average of $1.3 million in 1953-56 to an average of $3.0 million in 1957-60. While it is true that the amount of internally-held public debt is not a very serious matter, externally-held debt is so, and the amount of this is now large enough to pose future balance of payments problems when the country becomes independent.

Unfortunately there is almost no good information on the distribution of incomes among persons in British Guiana. Casual observation suggests that there is not that great gulf between rich and poor that marks so many under-developed countries, especially in Latin America. Large-scale conspicuous consumption is conspicuous mainly by its absence, and no shanty towns exist on the scale of West Kingston in Jamaica or of the swamps of Port of Spain in Trinidad. In 1960 only $22.7 million was liable for individual income tax, and was paid by 10,827 persons (income tax begins at around an income of $2000, depending on allowances). On the other hand, the strong seasonal element in many of the economic activities in B.G. means that there is probably much greater variation *within* the range of working class incomes than there is in, say, Jamaica or Trinidad.

The Structure of the Economy

The governing dynamic of the economy is provided by exports, and four main groups of products account

for by far the greatest part of these, as shown in Table 7.

TABLE 7. *Exports of selected commodities from British Guiana 1957–1960* (in millions of West Indian dollars)

	1957	1958	1959	1960	Average Percentage 1957–60
Sugar, molasses and rum	59·8	60·7	52·2	63·3	54·8
Rice	9·2	4·8	12·5	15·4	9·7
Metalliferous ores and metal scrap*	29·5	20·6	25·3	31·9	24·9
Timber	3·5	3·6	3·3	3·5	3·2
Other exports	5·1	6·7	8·7	11·0	7·3
Total domestic exports	107·1	96·4	102·0	125·1	100·0

*Note: Before 1959 this item refers to bauxite only. In 1959 bauxite exports alone were $24·8 million, compared to $25·3 million for this item. In 1960 manganese became important, and later—in 1961—alumina as well.

Sources: *Annual Report, British Guiana, 1961* (Georgetown, no date), p. 73, and *Quarterly Statistical Digest*, March 1962, Table 39.

Sugar and its by-products stayed fairly constant at around 55 per cent of exports, and rice rose steadily apart from the bad year of 1958, caused by the poor harvest of 1957. Similarly bauxite and other ores declined in 1958 with the U.S. recession but soon recovered. 'Other exports' increased at quite a rapid rate, especially fish, diamonds, and transport equipment, consisting mainly of boats.

Naturally these four activities of sugar, rice, mining and timber contained a smaller percentage of GDP than of exports, since all the background services of distribution and so on are also included in GDP. The following list shows the percentage contribution, on average, to GDP during the period 1957–60 by the main activities in the economy.[2]

[2] Calculated from Table 2.2 of A. Kundu, op. cit., *Social and Economic Studies*, September 1963. 'Other agriculture' includes such crops as coconuts, coffee, cocoa and citrus, as well as food crops like plantains (bananas) and root vegetables.

Sugar growing and milling	18·0%	Rice growing and milling	4·3%
Mining	7·7%	Forestry	5·2%
Livestock and fisheries	3·7%	Other agriculture, including processing	5·8%
Manufacturing, engineering chemicals	3·2%	Distribution	13·9%
Fuel, power and transport communications	8·2%	Banking and insurance	3·1%
Professions and personal service	5·9%	Building and construction	10·2%
Rent and dwellings	1·3%	Government	10·0%

Total 100·0%

Notice the relatively higher position assumed by forestry in GDP than in exports, mainly because much of its product goes into other domestic activities, such as construction, and so is not exported directly. Apart from processing of the main export crops, there is very little manufacturing (only 3.2 per cent). It will be convenient here to comment very briefly on the performance of three of the main activities during this period.

(a) *Sugar growing and milling:* Production rose fairly steadily from 240,000 tons in 1953 to 340,000 tons in 1960, with 327,000 tons of the latter being exported, 30,000 to the U.S.A. and the rest to Britain and Canada. Most of this expansion was accomplished by increasing the number of acres planted and reaped, since the yield of sugar per acre reaped changed only insignificantly, from 3.36 tons in 1953 to 3.47 tons in 1960.[3] But the number of workers in both field and factory fell substantially, from about 26,300 in 1953 to 20,500 in 1960, due chiefly to increased mechanisation. As a result, of course, output per man at work climbed substantially. In 1953, 100 acres under cane required about 27 field workers, in 1960 only 17; in 1953, 1000 tons of milled sugar needed

[3] These and all subsequent figures in this sub-section are calculated from data provided in E. P. Reubens and B. G. Reubens, op. cit. Chapter II.

24 factory workers, in 1960 only 13. Those workers who stayed in employment fared very well, since their average annual earnings rose from $585 in 1954 to $1085 or, in 'real' terms, by about two-thirds.

Not only did almost six thousand people lose their jobs in the sugar industry in this period of rapidly increasing population, but also the nature of the technical improvements was such that the seasonal fluctuations in employment have been exacerbated. The fall in employment itself was heaviest among females, youths and old men, and this may have mitigated its social consequences somewhat, but they are still serious. It is probably true that such increasing output per man is necessary if B.G. is to stay in the world sugar business, but it is certainly necessary that every effort should be made by the sugar estates and the Government to see that this is accomplished with as little distress as possible, retraining the labour which is released and finding it worthwhile jobs. It appears from the Reubens' report that these problems have not yet been satisfactorily solved by the authorities concerned.

(b) *Rice growing and milling:* Rice production increased considerably in this period, helped by the large investments in land drainage, irrigation and clearance of the Government's development schemes. Output rose from 75,000 tons in 1953 to 126,000 tons in 1960, and acreage from 112,500 to 220,207 acres during the same period. Yields per acre did not rise at all, the 1953-56 average being 0.58 tons and the 1958-60 average (leaving out the disastrous 1957 crop) being 0.55 tons.[4] There is a good deal of evidence that tractors and other mechanical appliances are used much more than formerly,[5] but this does not seem to have had much effect on yields, which implies

[4] Calculated from Reubens and Reubens, op. cit., p. 104. Paddy lands that were double-cropped are counted twice in this tabulation.
[5] Reubens and Reubens, loc. cit., and *Annual Report of the Director of Agriculture, 1961* (Georgetown, July 1962), p. 7 and p. 9.

that they have been used either for extending acreage, for displacing existing labour, or purely as symbols of prestige. Surpringly enough, it has not been Government policy to foster labour-intensive methods of cultivation (which are well suited for rice) but instead it has tended to encourage more mechanised practices, both through the 'demonstration effect' of its own entirely mechanised British Guiana Rice Development Company which farms 2600 acres, and through its credit and import policies. Such an approach seems to need serious re-examination in the light of Guiana's large current surplus of labour.

(c) *Mining:* During this period bauxite production remained fairly static, apart from the fluctuations induced by American and other recessions. In 1952 output was 2,426,000 metric tons of dried bauxite, and B.G. was thus the world's second largest producer, after Surinam with 3,224,000 tons. By 1956 she had slipped to third place with 2,521,000 tons, the first being Surinam with 3,483,000 and second Jamaica with 3,134,000. By 1960 Jamaica was easily first with 5,837,000 tons, the U.S.S.R. second with an estimated 3,500,000, Surinam third with 3,455,000 and B.G. fourth with 2,517,000 tons.[6] The phenomenal increase in Jamaican bauxite production was undoubtedly a major factor in her rapid economic growth over this period, and it is a pity that B.G. did not enjoy a similar experience. No doubt her rather high production costs, as well as her greater shipping costs—caused by longer distances from markets, and the sandbars on the Demerara and the Berbice—have put her at a disadvantage compared with Jamaica; as a partial recompense, manganese ore production began in 1960 and by 1961 reached 212,000 long tons.

[6] H. Bachmann: 'Aluminium as an Export Industry', a paper prepared for United Nations Conference on Trade and Development (February 1964), Annex, Table II. The Aluminium Company of Canada and Reynolds are active in Jamaica also, as is Kaiser Aluminum and—more recently—Alcoa, which operates in Surinam as well.

Employment and Unemployment

British Guiana, like most poor countries, does not have a regular count of its labour force, nor of its employed and unemployed, and it must therefore rely on the results of special surveys and on information collected as a by-product of a population census. During 1953–1960, there was one sample survey directed by Mr. McGale for the I.L.O. in 1956, and one census carried out in April 1960. Some of the main results of these two investigations are presented and compared in Table 8.

Let us deal with the 1956 survey first. For obvious reasons it was not expedient to cover the whole of B.G., and the actual survey area comprised most of the coastlands, covering an estimated 83.6 per cent of the population. Defining the labour force as those who 'were gainfully employed, or, if unemployed, were seeking work or wanted work', it estimated that 39.3 per cent of the population were in this category, with 51.0 per cent of the males in the the labour force and 28.3 per cent of the females. Remembering from Chapter III that about one half of the population was by 1960 either too young or too old to work, it follows that these participation rates indicate that almost all the males of working age, and just over half the females, were in the labour force.

The most startling result of the McGale survey was the high estimated percentage (18.0 per cent) of unemployment; a small repeat survey in September 1956, at a time of greater seasonal activity in the sugar industry, produced a somewhat lower figure of 16.4 per cent of the labour force. In neither case was the unemployment evenly divided between men and women. There were actually *more* unemployed women (15.2 thousand) than men (14.4 thousand) according to the July survey, even though only just over half the women of working age were in the labour force. The percentage of unemployed among males was 13.8 per cent, but among females was an enormous

TABLE 8. *Labour Force Statistics for British Guiana, 1956 and 1960*
(in thousands of persons unless otherwise stated)

	Survey Area July 1956	Survey Area April 1960	Whole of B.G. April 1960	Georgetown and environs July 1956	Georgetown and suburbs April 1960	Rest of Survey Area July 1956	Rest of Survey Area April 1960
1. Total population	418·3	468·5	560·4	121·3	148·4	297·0	320·1
(a) Male	204·2	233·4	279·2	56·8	69·9	147·4	164·5
(b) Female	214·1	235·1	281·2	64·5	78·5	149·6	156·6
2. Labour Force	164·6	146·3	175·0	49·9	52·1	114·7	94·2
(a) Male	104·1	112·1	134·1	30·5	34·3	73·6	77·8
(b) Female	60·5	34·2	40·9	19·4	17·8	41·1	16·4
3. Labour Force as percentage of population	39·3%	31·2%	31·2%	41·1%	35·1%	38·6%	29·4%
(a) Male	51·0%	48·0%	48·0%	53·7%	49·1%	49·9%	47·3%
(b) Female	28·3%	14·5%	14·5%	30·1%	22·6%	27·5%	10·5%
4. Numbers employed at time of investigation	135·0	130·5	156·1	38·8	45·6	96·2	84·9
(a) Male	89·7	101·1	120·9	25·8	30·8	63·9	70·3
(b) Female	45·3	29·5	35·3	13·0	14·8	32·3	14·6
5. Number unemployed	29·6	15·8	18·8	11·1	6·5	18·5	9·3
(a) Male	14·4	11·1	13·2	4·7	3·6	9·7	7·5
(b) Female	15·2	4·7	5·6	6·4	2·9	8·8	1·8
6. Unemployed as percentage of Labour Force	18·0%	10·8%	10·8%	22·2%	12·4%	16·1%	9·9%
(a) Male	13·8%	9·9%	9·9%	15·4%	10·3%	13·2%	9·7%
(b) Female	25·1%	13·7%	14·5%	33·0%	16·4%	21·4%	10·8%

Sources: For July 1956, *Report to the Government of British Guiana on Employment and Unemployment in the Colony in 1956* (Geneva, International Labour Office, 1957)—known as McGale Report:

For April 1960, Census Bulletin No. 19—'Labour Force by Sex and Work Status', *Population Census 1960, Series D, British Guiana,* (Port of Spain, Population Census Division, December 28, 1963).

25.1 per cent; in the September survey the corresponding figures were 11.2 per cent and 26.5 per cent, an even larger disparity.

If one now looks at the position in Georgetown, both because of its urban and racial character and because it has been the centre of so much unrest, it is clear that unemployment there (22.2 per cent) was significantly higher, especially among women (33.0 per cent compared with 25.1 per cent); similar percentages were obtained in the September survey, as one might have expected, since sugar is not important in Georgetown itself, nor in the inner suburbs. Outside Georgetown unemployment was correspondingly lower. The general picture then appeared to be of rural male unemployment at about 10 per cent in crop time, 13 per cent out of crop, and urban male unemployment at a steady 15 per cent. Rural female unemployment was about 21–24 per cent in or out of crop, and in the town was at the fantastic rate of 33 per cent. The male unemployment rates were certainly high, especially in the towns, but not out of line with the experience of many similar underdeveloped countries; the female rates are extremely high.

Let us now turn to the results of the 1960 Census, which was conducted in a month of high seasonal activity for the sugar industry, and in a year which—as we have seen—experienced considerable prosperity, the GDP increasing by about $12\frac{1}{2}$ per cent from the year before. Because the Census covered the whole country, we multiply the numerical results by 0.836 to bring them into line, very roughly, with those for the McGale survey area.[7]

[7] It should be stressed that this adjustment changes neither the labour force participation rates nor the unemployment rates obtained in the whole Census, since both numerator and denominator of these ratios are multiplied by the same factor of 0.836. The numerical results for Georgetown and district are not affected at all, since it was completely contained in the area of both investigations, although it is of course possible that there are minor differences in boundaries between the 'Georgetown and environs' of 1956 and the 'Georgetown and suburbs' of 1960.

The most striking aspect of these new results is the much lower participation rate (31.2 per cent) and unemployment rate (10.8 per cent) in 1960 compared to the corresponding 1956 figures of 39.3 per cent and 18.0 per cent. But on closer examination the rates for the males alone do not appear to differ very much, and the discrepancies could probably be accounted for by sampling and enumeration errors, and by the greater prosperity in 1960. The rates for women are quite different however, the labour force participation rate in 1960 being just over half that in 1956, and similarly with the unemployment rate. The total number of women in the labour force apparently fell from 60.5 thousand in 1956 to an estimated 34.2 thousand in 1960, even though population increased by 12 per cent over this period.

Clearly there must be some difference in concept between the two investigations, since even though we know that the employment of women may well have fallen (as in the sugar industry), it is not conceivable that half the female labour force just quit. The answer seems to be as follows: in 1956, the 'labour force' consisted of people who were in work, or who were unemployed or who *wanted* work; in 1960, the 'labour force' consisted of those who were at work at any time in the preceding year or *whose main activity* was seeking work. Especially for women with families, there is however a world of difference between being prepared to accept an attractive job if it is offered, and actually looking hard every day for one. The latter concept is a better measure of the *social* problem of unemployment, while the former is rather a measure of unused human capacity in the economy.

For these reasons I am inclined to accept the Census figures as being preferable to those of the Survey, at least for purposes of current social and economic policy; of course neither set of estimates is really satisfactory. Notice that the Census showed proportionately much lower urban unemployment in 1960 than in 1956, a difference

of ten percentage points, and further that there was little difference between urban and rural unemployment rates for men, though a major difference between those for women (16.4 per cent to 10.8 per cent). If correct, these findings materially alter the validity of earlier comments which called attention to the implications of the much higher rates of unemployment in the towns, and which were based on the McGale survey.[8]

2. The Period 1961–1963: General Trends

It is very difficult to find good data on the progress of the economy in the last three years, and Table 9 pulls together from various sources most of the quantitative information on general trends which seems to be available, at least to someone writing outside British Guiana.

TABLE 9. Indicators of Economic Trends in British Guiana 1961–1963

(all figures in millions of West Indian dollars, unless otherwise stated; n.a. indicates not available)

	1961	1962	1963
1. Gross Domestic Product at factor cost	255·7	250	250
2. Value of sugar exports (including by-products)	62·6	65	n.a.
3. Value of rice exports	22·6	23	n.a.
4. Value of exports of metalliferous ores and metal scrap	46·1	54	n.a.
5. Value of total exports	146·5	155	165
6. Value of total imports	147·0	128	125
7. Quantity of sugar exported ('000 tons)	310	310	290
8. Quantity of bauxite exported ('000 tons)	2374*	1800	1100
9. Quantity of alumina exported ('000 tons)	116*	210	220
10. Consumer Price Index (1956=100) in June of each year (%)	107·2	109·8	n.a.

Sources: Annual Report, British Guiana, 1961.
Budget Speeches, 1962, 1963, 1964.
Quarterly Statistical Digest, September 1962, Table 13.

Note: *Production, not exports.

[8] See, for example, Peter Newman: 'Racial Tension in British Guiana', *Race*, Vol. 3, May 1962, p. 38.

Not too much importance should be attached to the estimates of GDP, since it is clear from the Budget Speeches in which the last two were given that they are to be understood as orders of magnitude only. Taken literally, the 1963 figure would imply a considerable fall in GDP *per capita* from 1960 (when total GDP was $270 million), for population has increased by 9 per cent–10 per cent since then and prices by probably about 5 per cent; this of course may well have happened, but there is simply not enough information to prove it one way or another. Sugar exports fell slightly from the record 1960 level in 1961, kept even to 1962, and then fell again in 1963, due to labour troubles which are discussed in the next chapter. The enormous rise in the world price of sugar in 1963 (from £22.2 a ton in 1962 to an average of £67.2 in 1963) must have made this fall in quantity hard to bear, since the loss of 20,000 tons would have fetched at least £6.5 million on the free market, B.G's Commonwealth Sugar Agreement quota having already been met.

The considerable loss of confidence during 1962 in the sectors producing for home consumption is shown in the fall in imports from 1961 to 1962, and they declined a little more even in 1963, when one might have expected an increase to replenish stocks run down in 1962. The fall in quantity of bauxite from 1961 to 1962 is partly but not wholly accounted for by the increasing production of alumina, but that cannot explain the drastic fall of 1963, probably again occasioned by labour troubles. Rice exports on the other hand seem to have kept up fairly well, with substantial shipments to Cuba and Russia as well as to the usual West Indian markets.

The general picture, based on the very sketchy information available, is of general stagnation over the last three years, which would probably have led to an outright decline in 1963 if it had not been for the very welcome rise in sugar prices. As it was, it is probable that *per capita*

incomes probably declined by about 10 per cent from 1960, and that unemployment increased significantly during the same period.

The Development Programme

Beginning in January 1960 the Government embarked on a Development Programme for the next five years, which is therefore due to finish at the end of 1964. Drawn up on the advice of a Cambridge economist, Mr. Kenneth Berrill, it was more a loose collection of assorted Government projects, many of them concerned with drainage and irrigation to benefit paddy lands, than a coherent economic plan in the modern sense of the term, i.e. a plan embracing the private sector as well, with a clearly de-defined set of targets based on a long-run perspective.[9]

The distribution of this public investment programme, and of the earlier one from 1956 to 1959, has been of considerable economic and political significance. In a rather detailed paper written at the start of the pro-gramme,[10] it was argued that the allocation of funds was not in fact such as to promote rapid economic growth. Some 53 per cent of the planned expenditure for 1960–64 was for agriculture, and within agriculture most of this was for rice land projects, which have a very low yield on capital invested, both in economic terms and in narrower financial terms; it has been estimated that the return to Government from some of the major rice projects is not more than 3.1 per cent whereas the rate of interest at which much of the money is borrowed is around 6 per cent.[11]

Since it is mainly East Indians who are rice farmers, there is little doubt that the Programme in effect represented

[9] See Development Programme 1960–1964 (Sessional Paper No. 5/1959), and K. Berrill: Report on the British Guiana Development Programme 1960–1964 (Sessional Paper No. 2/1960).
[10] Peter Newman: 'The Economic Future of British Guiana', Social and Economic Studies, Vol. 9, September 1960, pp. 263–296.
[11] British Guiana: Report on the Financial Position, by K. C. Jacobs (H.M.S.O. Colonial No. 358, 1964), Appendix 2.

some transfer of income from the urban, predominantly
Negro and Mixed areas, to the rural areas which are much
more heavily Indian, and it might be thought that such an
expenditure pattern therefore reflects the chiefly Indian
support for Dr. Jagan's majority party. Some element of
this was present in the investment decisions, but a much
more important factor in the situation was one of poor
economic planning. Given a lack of any kind of economic
planning staff, and a dearth of skilled agricultural and
industrial engineers who could examine projects carefully,
there was a natural tendency to concentrate on those
projects of irrigation and drainage for rice which had been
on the drawing board for several years. Almost no attempt
seems to have been made to go into the economic feasibility
of the rice schemes, or very seriously into the possibilities
of diversification into other crops which might yield a
higher income, and so help to recoup the cost of the investment. Although two years after the Programme came into
operation an economic planning unit was assembled,
there is yet really no sign that the Government administration understands the crucial importance of correct allocation of investment funds. When Dr. Jagan tours many
countries with his urgent requests for economic aid for
his development programmes, his case is seriously
handicapped because his 'programmes' are not the well-
thought-out integrated plans they should be, designed to
raise the living standards of the whole people as quickly
as possible, but are rather a collection of departmental
projects hurriedly thrown together to impress aid-granting
countries. This is not to say that the Government's concern
with development is not sincere, for it is—with most
ministers at least—but the essential *seriousness* of economic
development does not seem to have yet penetrated the
current administration.

From 1956 to 1959 the public investment programme
ran at an average level of $19.3 million, which was about

9 per cent of GDP. The planned rate for 1960–64 was
$22.1 million, beginning around $25 million in 1960
and trailing off to $19 million by 1964. Whether this
planned rate was too low or too high is a question that
cannot really be answered, since there was so little information on prospective investment projects. The sluggish
rate of economic growth of about 3 per cent seems *prima
facie* evidence that it is too low, though the Programme
was drawn up on the assumption that the real rate of
growth of G.D.P. had recently been and would continue
to be at 6 per cent, irrespective of the size and allocation of
the public investment.

Even the low level of the actual programme constituted a
sufficiently heavy burden on the economy that the Government felt itself unable to finance more than a fraction of
the planned expenditure. During 1955–59 only $10 million
was raised from revenue surpluses, out of a total public
development expenditure of about $100 million.   For
1960–64 it was planned to raise $15 million from revenue
surpluses and $10 million from local borrowing, in order to
help finance a total of $110 million; of the balance
$23 million was to be in outright grants from the British
Government, and about $38 million was to be in the form
of exchequer loans. It was hoped that the gap of $23 million
would be filled by international grants and loans and by
underspending.

At the beginning of the Programme the announced
reluctance to tax adequately was even more marked in
practice, for the first year began with a revenue surplus of
only $1.1 million, merely a third of what had been planned.
It soon became apparent that taxes would have to be
raised to provide higher surpluses, especially as the hoped-
for international grants and loans were not materialising
at all. After its election to office in August 1961, the Jagan
Government in its first Budget courageously attempted
to increase substantially the locally-raised funds for

development, to a level above that envisaged by the original Programme. Devised by another Cambridge economist, the very distinguished Dr. Nicholas Kaldor, the new revenue proposals were an ingenious package consisting of higher rates for old taxes (e.g. import duties), new taxes (e.g. capital gains taxes) and a scheme for compulsory private saving.

It was these proposals (as we shall see) that led directly to the grave riots of February 1962, and it is ironic that the first serious attempt to make the Guianese responsible for their own development should have caused such a tear in the fabric of the society. But before condemning this violent reaction completely—and the behaviour of the Opposition leaders was quite shockingly irresponsible— —it must be remembered that a national economic plan should plan its expenditure fairly and productively so that the great mass of the people benefit, and clearly realise that they benefit; and this the 1960-64 Programme conspicuously failed to do. It should have been the task of the Government and its advisers to ensure that the money that was to be raised by such heavy taxation was well and fairly spent, and so to devote as much ingenuity to revenue spending as to revenue raising; and the task of the Opposition to assist constructively but critically in these tasks. Both sides failed badly.

As it happened, some of the new revenue proposals were withdrawn, and others have proved administratively very difficult to implement. In the last three years B.G. has had chronic difficulties with the Programme, caused by financial stringency and the practical problems of implementation. Table 10 provides a progress report on the Development Programme since its inception, from which can be seen a recurring pattern of high initial estimates, lowered revised estimates (except in 1961, following the boom year 1960), and actual expenditure at a yet lower level.

TABLE 10. *Progress of the Development Programme 1960–1964*
(all figures in millions of West Indian dollars; n.a. indicates not available)

	1960	1961	1962	1963	1964	Total
1. Original Development Plan Estimates	24·8	22·7	23·7	20·4	18·9	110·5
2. Revised to take account of under-estimation and increased cost of materials and labour	n.a.	n.a.	n.a.	n.a.	n.a.	135·0
3. Development Estimates 1960	24·7					
4. Budget Speech Revision 1960	22·1					
5. Actual Expenditure 1960	15·8					
6. Development Estimates 1961		24·0				
7. Revised estimates 1961, including supplementary votes		31·6				
8. Actual expenditure 1961		21·6				
9. Development Estimates 1962			31·6			
10. Budget Speech Revision 1962			20·0			
11. Actual Expenditure 1962 (provisional estimate)			18·8			
12. Development Estimates 1963				25·5		
13. Budget Speech Revision 1963				17·6		
14. Actual Expenditure 1963 (provisional estimate)				12·3		
15. Development Estimates 1964					20·7	
16. Budget Speech Revision 1964					13·7	
17. Actual (1960–63) or planned (1964) Expenditure	15·8	21·6	18·8	12·3	13·7	82·2

Sources: *Development Programme, 1960–1964* (Sessional Paper No. 5/1959).
    Development Estimates, 1960 and 1963.
    Budget Speeches, 1960, 1962, 1963, 1964.
    Report of the Accountant General for the year 1961.
    British Guiana: Report on the Financial Position, by K. C. Jacobs (H.M.S.O., Colonial No. 358, 1964).
    Statement by the Government of British Guiana on the Jacobs Report (Sessional Paper No. 1/1964).

The original Programme of $110.5 million was revised upwards in early 1962 to $135.0 million to take account not of increased scope, but of rises in prices and of under-costing of several of the projects. In the event not more than $82.2 million, or not quite 61 per cent of the original Programme, will have been spent by the end of 1964, a rate of public investment substantially lower ($16.5 million in 1960–64 compared to $19.3 million) than that of the earlier Programme for 1956–59. As with the development of general economic trends since 1960, it is difficult to resist the impression of an economy that is stagnating and is even in serious danger of running down, unless vigorous steps are soon taken to check the present drift.

The Future of Foreign Enterprises

Before moving on to discuss Guianese politics in the last chapter, it is useful to consider briefly—and without giving any specific answers—a problem which lies at the borderland of economics with politics. What is to be the future of the foreign businesses which at present control the Guianese economy? Are they to be left to their own devices, are they to be nationalised or what is to become of them?

The salient feature of these firms is that they operate on a very large scale, both in relation to the Guianese economy and society, and absolutely; and it is unlikely that they could operate on a smaller scale without serious economic loss. Chapter I has shown that the nature of sugar cultivation on the coastlands necessarily encourages large scale production, so that only two firms, Bookers and Sandbach Parker, now control the entire industry. Similarly large scale is necessary in bauxite and manganese mining, which the Demerara Bauxite company (Alcan), Reynolds Metals and the North West Guiana Mining Company control. These five firms together account for nearly 80

per cent of British Guiana's exports, which total around £30 million a year. Moreover, it is unlikely that future industrialisation, based as it probably will be on hydro-electric power, will be much smaller in scale if it is to be efficient.

The domination of the economy by a few companies is bound to produce local views of the 'free enterprise' system at variance with the highly competitive, property-owning, profit-sharing democracy idealised by Western moderates, even though in recent years the larger companies —expecially Bookers—have had some enlightened leader-ship, not always effectively implemented at operational level. The point is not that the companies are exploiting monopoly capitalists—which is true in some senses and not in others—but that they are so *large* relative to Guianese society that individual members of the society necessarily feel alienated from the main stream of economic life. In such conditions there naturally arises a demand for national ownership and control of these businesses, but again the much smaller scale of the Guianese society as a whole makes these demands unrealistic as a short-run aim; it will be a long time before the Guianese civil service has sufficient staff and training to enforce effective detailed control of such enormous organisations.

This dilemma sets up tensions which are a long way from being resolved. The radicals feel frustrated since nationali-sation cannot be accomplished soon, and in their frustration develop an 'all or nothing attitude', tending to overlook possible steps that could be taken towards public partici-pation and control. The capitalists, on the other hand, are naturally somewhat inhibited from pursuing a policy of aggressive expansion, partly because of the risk of nationa-lisation and partly because they do not wish to loom even larger in Guianese society. Bookers in particular are trying hard to become relatively less important—or at least less noticeable—by diversifying both within and

outside British Guiana.[12] But to shrink deliberately is not a simple thing to do, especially in a country laying emphasis on the need for economic expansion.

It would be a serious mistake if these tensions were not resolved. First, it is quite essential that the Guianese be given a much greater sense of participation in their own economic destiny, and this requires that in some way or other the public interest should be associated—not necessarily wholly—with the ownership and control of these large enterprises. Secondly, in a society where there is so little organisational capacity as there is in B.G. at present, and where the nature of the country requires large-scale operations, it is equally essential that such loci of organisation as Bookers should not be broken up or run down, but should remain as instruments by which to advance rapid economic progress, working in complete harmony with the Government and perhaps on activities that have so far lain outside their range of interests. A good economic organisation should be able to turn its talents to the production of any one of a surprising range of commodities.

[12] This diversification overseas has led Bookers into quite unrelated industries, such as automobile spare parts in Western Canada. Perhaps the most bizarre move in this direction is their recent purchase of a 51 per cent interest in the copyright of all books by Ian Fleming, the creator of James Bond (see *Atticus* in the *Sunday Times*, 22 March 1964).

V. POLITICAL DEVELOPMENTS
1953—1963

It is scarcely surprising that the past and present forms of social and economic organisation—in essence that of one giant plantation—should have stimulated many Guianese to seek radical solutions to the deep and stultifying problems which faced them. This common left-wing direction, together with the circumstances that many of them were trained abroad, where other differences were often ignored (as with so many colonial students) in face of the strangeness and frequent hostility of the British or North American environment, acted to bring together the young East Indian and Negro politicians in a united front against the imperial régime.

This identification of interests was reinforced by the reactionary tendencies of the urban light-skinned middle classes, who had for many years tried to maintain a deep social gulf between themselves and the mass of the urban Negro population. This creole bourgeoisie was strongly in favour of the *status quo;* indeed the development of creole society had been such that it was difficult for its '*élite*' ever to imagine what a fully independent Guiana might be like, let alone to conceive of making the necessary adjustments in their ways of life and modes of thought to accommodate such a dash to the loneliness of freedom. Accordingly, apart from a few minor political parties such as the National Labour Front of Lionel Luckhoo (most conservative West Indian parties have a 'Labour' label, one of their more endearing oddities), the creole middle-classes did not have effective political representation before 1960, preferring to rely on the protection afforded by the nominated members of the Legislative Council, and on the strong residual powers of the Governor and the Colonial

Civil Service officials. Ultimately, perhaps, they depended
on the reasoning that the political influence exerted in
the metropolis by Big Business, especially Big Sugar,
would never allow B.G. to move further out of the British
orbit than, say, Jamaica or Trinidad have moved.

In any event, their strong opposition to social and political
reforms of even the mildest kind was a major force in the
unification of the Negro and the East Indian working-classes.
On the other side of the bourgeoisie, the non-creole side,
the large, prosperous and mainly rural Indian middle
classes were not in sympathy with the extremist tendencies
of the Indian left, but went along with it partly because of
racial affinity and Jagan's effective leadership, and partly
through dislike of the socially dominant and exclusive
urban creole group.

The last decade has seen the gradual break-up of the
united East Indian and Negro working-class opposition
to colonial rule. In its place, on the one hand, has been
the near alliance of the urbanised Negro proletariat with
the urban multi-racial bourgeoisie, and on the other the
greater cohesion between East Indian estate workers and
rice farmers, with the latter group gaining an increasing
say in political direction, especially as their numbers and
affluence have grown as a result of the Government's
paddy lands development programme. The net effect
has been to moderate in both groups the original radical
drives of the united front, although this moderation has been
obscured in the East Indian case by the extremism of
some of the party's pronouncements.

These developments need not have occurred. It is
possible to conceive that the united workers' front would
have persisted and induced in its turn a coalition of the
urban creole and rural East Indian middle-classes, resulting
in a fairly straightforward class struggle of the usual type.
This would no doubt have produced tensions, but the
society would probably have remained fairly coherent
and given the tendency to creolisation of the East Indians

(already remarked at the end of Chapter III), it would have become increasingly integrated, capable of an independent and reasonably stable political and economic life. The pattern which has in fact developed is disastrous. The coming together of the two sections of the creole society on the one hand, and of East Indian society on the other, has increasingly produced a clear split down the middle of Guianese life, polarising a society which was otherwise slowly moving towards integration into two opposed groups, the creoles and the East Indians.

In the next few pages we shall examine briefly how these tragic developments have come about. It is no part of the purpose to apportion blame for the present miserable situation, for the straightforward narrative should make it quite clear that ineptitude and lack of foresight was displayed by every side, including the colonial power. Even now, however, it is not too late to retrieve the position; the racial divisions do not yet run so deep nor are yet so ingrained as to prevent all possibility of reconciliation, while the forces making for integration are slow but sure, provided that political and economic policy allows them to come into play once more. The situation clearly calls for courageous and humane leadership to pull the two sides together in the increasingly urgent task of genuine economic development.   The example of Jomo Kenyatta's superb handling of the basically far more difficult Kenyan situation is an indication of what can be done by the exercise of true leadership. It is the most depressing aspect of British Guiana at present that leadership even remotely approaching such stature is nowhere in evidence, on any side.

1953 and After

It would take us too far afield to examine the 1953 political crisis in any detail, particularly since it has been well discussed elsewhere[1], but as it was one of the two major

[1] See Chapter VII of Raymond Smith, op. cit., which also includes a good analysis of political parties before 1953.

recent landmarks in Guianese politics (the other—in my judgement—being the riots of February 1962), and because it set the stage for most of what follows, it is necessary to give a short account.

The 'Waddington Constitution' of 1953 marked a substantial step forward on the road to independence, but still fell far short of true self-government. The young men and women of the People's Progressive Party (PPP), which was the the political expression of the united working-class front and of the Indian farmers, were naturally in a hurry to gain independence as soon as possible and took the fateful decision to seize every possible opportunity, while remaining as the legally elected Government, to show in their day-to-day activities that the interim constitution was unworkable, and so to force the colonial power to grant a more far-reaching formula for self-government. This decision was understandable but unwise, the work of clever but inexperienced politicians, for its precedent of acting in an essentially unconstitutional (if legal) manner augured badly for the future, which has suffered from much worse unconstitutional action since then.

If the PPP's policy was ill-advised, what can we say of the extreme reaction by the British Government in suspending the constitution, putting in a nominated Government and jailing several of the members of the former administration? Its recklessness can only be explained in terms of the anti-Communist hysteria of those McCarthy-ridden years, and by the first flush of the then recent Conservative Government, before its chastening by Suez. The evidence that the new ministers in B.G. had misbehaved, in such things as fomenting strikes and in trying to remove the ban on the entry of Communists and of Communist literature, while certainly proof that the PPP was not playing the game by the unwritten Colonial Office rules for decolonisation, was surely not enough to warrant the deeply

frustrating act of setting back the path to responsibility by several years. Less stringent measures would have sufficed.

As it was, the suppression of the constitution went too far and stayed too long, in this respect being reminiscent of the similar abrogation in Jamaica after the Morant Bay riots of 1865, which abolished the local legislative body and introduced Crown Colony government. The net effect of the 1953 intervention was to postpone for a long time the development of responsible thought about the real economic and social problems of the country, and therefore to move the locus of discussion back to constitutional problems of independence and eventually to problems of racial division, increasing those cross-currents of race and ideology that make the balanced elucidation of Guiana's politics so difficult.

Moreover the setback of 1953 led directly to the split early in 1955 between the Jaganite and Burnhamite factions of the PPP, a split which was to have such unfortunate consequences. It is difficult to find a fully adequate explanation for this fission in the leadership. One version sees it mainly as a struggle for personal position, with Burnham perceiving that he would stand a greater chance of accommodation with the imperial power if he was seen to be less uncompromising than the Jagan group. This explanation in terms of personal rivalry is reinforced by the consideration that ideologically the two factions remained close together, at least for some time, both being far out at the left end of the spectrum and both firmly committed to independence with all possible—and not merely all due—speed.

Another interpretation, not inconsistent with the first, attributes the split to the lack of organic unity in the Negro-East Indian coalition in the PPP, which could probably have been remedied if the party had gone on to real nation-building, but which was quickly revealed when further progress was blocked by the rape of the

constitution. This aspect was well analysed in the following quotation:[2]

The fact is that the PPP of 1953 had never been a homogeneous unit but a coalition. It had come together to spearhead the final attack on the imperial power and had had to set out the elements (but only the elements) of a universalistic vision ('socialism') so as to energise the latent drives of the colonial people. Nothing had to be stated . . . too precisely. Every man in the street knew after 450 years [of New World colonialism] who the real enemy was and what had to be done. The leaders had no serious problem in bringing the disparate sections together. But following from the colonial condition itself the unintegrated nature of the movement (due to economic specialisation, imperial population policy, differential acculturation) was a naked fact which did not have to be stated. Everybody knew it was a coalition. This PPP coalition was only a factor hastening the unification process which the internal and unconscious dynamics of the imperial system (e.g. deculturation of immigrants and exertion of social pressure on them to 'dignify' themselves by aping European culture and behaviour patterns) had started. *The coalition represented an advance along the road to unity, it was not a unity* [italics in original].

The very loosely defined 'socialism' referred to above continued to be a feature of the programme of both parts of the PPP after the split. The Jaganite faction maintained a fairly intransigent if vague Marxist position on economic policy, a position with which not all the party was entirely happy; but many were, and the political organisation formed and directed by Dr. and Mrs. Jagan (who acted as party secretary) was highly effective. Even its re-entry into Government in 1957 did not seriously moderate this

[2] *New World* (Georgetown, March 1963) pp. 6–7. This 100-page first issue of this intellectual magazine was wholly devoted to a most penetrating left-wing analysis of the problems facing B.G., though there are some youthful *naïvetés* (e.g. the cover contains a stirring poem by Aimé Césaire, the French West Indian apostle of '*négritude*', this in a magazine devoted to the integration of Negro and East Indian society!). It is regrettable—and symptomatic of Guiana's problems—that apparently there has been no subsequent issue, though it was promised as a quarterly journal.

position, since the power of the elected ministers under the
new constitution was not sufficiently real—even less so than
in 1953—for the worrisome responsibilities of administration to temper the doctrinaire party approach, though
both Jagan and his wife proved quite good administrators
within their restricted opportunities. Inconsistencies and
ambiguities in the party platform were allowed to remain—
and still do—so that on many important questions the
electorate has for long been unsure and distrustful of what
the party intends. This is not surprising, for many of the
leaders themselves seem not clear as to the type of society
and economy which they wish to bring about. Too many
of them, including even on occasion Jagan himself, are
given to making off-the-cuff speeches that are not consistent
with the image of a vigorous-but-fair, Marxist-but-demo-
cratic Government which they apparently wish to project
among the voters at large; such speeches quickly undo
any good repute that quiet administration might have
built up.

One of the most damning consequences of colonialism
as it has manifested itself in B.G., particularly with the
domination of the society by a few giant firms, is the set
of curiously complex attitudes of irresponsibility that many
of the leaders in all parties display, attitudes in contrast
with those demonstrated by many nationalist groups in
former colonial territories. It would take a deeper psychological analysis than is possible here to unravel this problem,
but it would seem that the habits of personal and economic
dependence enjoined by such large enterprises in a small
economy, and by the creole estate tradition, have produced
what for want of a better cliché might be described as a
love-hate relationship of the nationalists towards the
British Raj and towards Big Business. On the one hand it
gives the enjoyable feeling of being deliciously naughty
and daring to agitate in extreme left-wing or reactionary
terms against colonial authority, on the other they are
loath to embark firmly upon the difficult constructive

tasks of nation-building that must underpin true independence. The net effect has been to deny to the people the
responsible leadership which they need if they are ever to
escape the adverse consequences of their colonial origins.

An example of this type of politican, though certainly a
long way from the worst, is Dr. Jagan himself. Although for
long intervals he concerns himself mainly with the problems
of administering his country, the eagerness with which
at the end of those intervals he launches into denunciation
of the machinations of the imperialists indicates that he
is still happier as a party activist than he is as a national
leader. Dr. Smith has put a closely related point with
extremely subtlety:

When Dr Jagan says that he is a Marxist but not a member of the
Communist Party he is perhaps expressing his desire to accept
some of the main principles of communist political philosophy
without worrying too much about the implications of its application in the real world. It is evident that in the present state of
world power politics it is not possible to ignore the practical
implications of ideological commitment . . .[3]

Indicative of this attitude is Dr. Jagan's approach to the
recruitment of economic planners, whom he has tried to
obtain from very left-wing circles in western countries
and moderate under-developed countries, such as India.
In the nature of the case, such people (like Dr. Jagan)
have had little experience of responsibility for actually
planning the welfare of a nation. It would have been
preferable therefore to have tried to obtain economic
planners from Eastern European countries, such as Poland
and Yugoslavia, which have at least had some success—
and often considerable success—in actually devising and
carrying out a coherent plan.

It is possible to use this 'psychological' explanation of
the leadership for the relative inactivity that the Jagan-led
ministers displayed in their period of modest power from

[3] Raymond Smith, op. cit., p. 205.

1957 to 1961, when far from repeating their mistake of
1953 they did not use fully even the limited powers of the
1957 constitution to press home a strong drive for economic
and social development. This reluctance to govern as far
as they were able may also have been assisted by a feeling
among the party leaders that the world power struggle
might soon reach a point which would permit Guiana
to develop in a thoroughgoing Marxist fashion, with considerable help from the Socialist block and without inter-
ference from North America, so that in the meantime not
much more than a holding operation was necessary.
This I have earlier called the 'Waiting for Godot' solution[4],
and if it was a factor in PPP thinking it clearly represented
a gamble involving some risk with the economic progress
of the people.

The public ideology of the predominantly Negro
Burnhamite opposition, which became the People's National
Congress (PNC) after the election of 1957, was—as we
have remarked—close to that of Jagan's group, although
the latter was generally regarded as the true fount fo
socialist doctrine. This adherence of both groups to 'universalistic socialism' stemmed from genuine personal
conviction, from electoral considerations and from the
lack of any serious responsibility—as Government or
Opposition—for important policy decisions, which allowed
quite unrealistic ideas about available possibilities to persist
unchanged.

The overt position of the two factions in the 1957 elections
had both been sternly against racial issues, but in the grass-
roots campaign these issues became important on both sides.
The defeat of the Burnham-led group in this campaign
resulted in an increased emphasis on Negro race conscious-
ness. Haunted by the higher rates of East Indian population
growth, which would clearly place them within ten years

[4] Peter Newman: 'Epilogue on British Guiana', *Social and Economic
Studies*, Vol. 10, March 1961, pp. 35-41.

or so in an absolute electoral as well as an absolute population majority, it tried to create a Negro solidarity that
would, it hoped, prevail at the polls against the more
numerous Indians, especially since some of the latter
might not vote with the PPP. This policy of the PNC was
amazingly shortsighted. Even assuming (and it is a big
assumption) that it had succeeded in the short run, it
would only have done so at the cost of arousing implacable
East Indian opposition, and given the latter's clear
lead in population growth this would eventually have
driven the Negroes from any future chance of political
power. These demographic facts were well-known and it
seems obvious that the correct policy for the PNC, of all
parties, should have been to seek a *rapprochement* with the
East Indians, hastening the natural process of their creolisation rather than rejecting them outright. That the PNC
leaders did not follow such a policy can only be explained
by a gross miscalculation on their part, perhaps aided—
consciously or unconsciously—by the unwarranted scorn
of many creoles for 'coolie culture'.

As time went on the PNC became both more extreme
on the racial issue and more moderate on the issue of
socialism, and both these tendencies were reinforced by
its absorption of the United Democratic Party, which
had been the political wing of the League of Coloured
Peoples, a mainly middle-class Negro pressure group;
both John Carter and W. O. R. Kendall, leaders of this
party, were and are essentially conservative in ideology.
But there was an ultimate barrier to the extent to which the
PNC could move rightwards, formed by the political
views of the urban creole '*élite*'. Any identification of the
PNC with this group at this period would have meant the
alienation of many of the Negro proletariat, in addition
to being personally objectionable to most of the Negro
leaders of the party.

Not surprisingly, this attention to a unified Negro front
including the darker middles classes as well, principally

civil servants and teachers, led to the need for a common enemy, a role which was increasingly filled by the East Indians. Operating within its restricted social and economic framework, and with the initiative on 'socialism' and independence resting mainly with the PPP, the chief animus of the PNC was focused on the racial issue, and even official party pronouncements began to take on a racial tinge. Since the PPP continued to maintain a public image of non-racialism (although its local support was often less unbiased, as Indian rice farmers increasingly became an important element of the party) many Negro intellectuals, especially among the younger group, began to feel dissatisfied with the racial policies of the PNC. Except in a few cases this did not lead them to the PPP, but it did cause them to withold their active participation in the Negro party. Partly as a result the second-rank leadership of the PNC has tended in the past to be less able than the corresponding echelons of the PPP, though in recent years this tendency has lessened as the latter party has also lost some of its stronger members, some going to the PNC or other parties, and others dropping out of active politics altogether.

The Election of 1961[5]

The prospect of a new interim constitution amounting to almost complete self-government, to take effect in 1961 after elections to be held in August, and to be followed very soon—it was thought—by complete independence, spurred the formation in November 1960 of a new middle-class party, the United Force (UF). This was mainly the creation of an energetic Georgetown business-man of

[5] For a good account of the progress of this election, see C. Paul Bradley: 'The Party System in British Guiana and the General Election of 1961', *Caribbean Studies* (University of Puerto Rico, Institute of Caribbean Studies), Vol. 1, October 1961, pp. 1–26. His forecasts of future developments have not however proved correct, B.G. so far being a long way from a one-party state, on either the Socialist model or the African model.

Portuguese Catholic descent, Peter D'Aguiar, and drew to itself the multi-racial but deeply conservative creole middle-classes of British Guiana; the immediate occasion of its formation was to protest against a greater degree of State control of the church primary schools, which are financed by the State but run by individual churches, both Protestant and Catholic.

Because of the position of the PPP and the PNC out on the left, there was an 'opening to the centre' which the basically right-wing UF hastened to fill; its announced grandiose programme of economic development was very vague in its details and was probably further to the left than its architects and main supporters had any real intention of being, if and when they attained office. Although few of its candidates were of any stature the United Force fought each constituency with a lavishly equipped campaign. The sources of its funds are obscure, although D'Aguiar is himself fairly wealthy, as are many of his supporters. His strong, indeed hysterical anti-Communist line may have attracted private funds from abroad—it certainly attracted Dr. Fred Schwartz's Anti-Communist Crusade, with mobile film units and plenty of right-wing literature; there was also a dash of Moral Rearmament, to add flavour to the mixture.

Despite the support from the Press (one of the newspapers, the most irresponsible, is owned by D'Aguiar), and strong though unofficial support from the Catholic and Anglican churches, the UF could count on few popular votes, except in the richer districts of Georgetown and among the Amerindian population, where the influence of Catholic missions was important. It is important to note that the middle-classes' implicit reliance on Big Business proved a broken reed, for the really big firms kept a carefully neutral position in politics, the biggest of them all, Bookers —under the direction of its socialist chairman Sir Jock Campbell—making it fairly clear that it was not prepared to support the UF. As a result the UF has increasingly vented some of its plentiful spleen on 'expatriate' Big Business,

accusing its directors of living in complacency far away from the turmoil of B.G., while the local smaller business-men are manfully upholding the banner of capitalism under desperate conditions.   Their criticism of such foreign firms is at least as violent as that of the left-wing parties, and adds yet another paradox to the Guianese situation.

The question arises, why did the United Force fight the election when it had such a small chance of success? It is strongly arguable that the existence of UF rather than PPP candidates in Georgetown consolidated the anti-PNC vote there and so forced the PNC to fight hard in its normal metropolitan stronghold, thus reducing its efforts in the marginal areas. This resulted in the anti-PPP vote being split seriously enough to allow Jagan to come to office. Since the PNC was less extreme on economic policy than the PPP, and increasingly so, why did the UF not settle for the Negro party as the lesser evil? It is under-standable that a centre party might try to get votes from either wing, as the Liberals try to do in England, but the UF is not really a centre party.

Three probable reasons can be distinguished; the fact that they are largely inconsistent with each other need not, in this context, lessen their validity. The first is that D'Aguiar genuinely believed that his party would triumph (twenty-three of its thirty-five candidates lost their deposits and only four of them, including D'Aguiar, won seats); in the heat of the emotional fervour accompanying the birth of the party, this dream might not have seemed unrealistic. The second reason lies in the traditional disdain in which the urban middle-class hold the Negro proletariat, and in its more defensible dislike of the racialism of the PNC. Seen in this light, the People's National Congress was not a lesser evil than the People's Progressive Party, in spite of the former's less extreme economic radicalism. Many people in Georgetown who voted UF preferred the PPP at that time to the PNC; and conversely the United

Force embodied for many poor Negroes social attitudes which were far worse than those of the less ideologically distant party led by Jagan.

The third reason is simply that the United Force probably did not initially envisage fighting the election alone at all. Early in the campaign there were negotiations to bring together the UF and the PNC on one solid anti-Jagan ticket, but these foundered mainly on the question of the distribution of office should the coalition be successful. By the time these negotiations failed the UF had to fight or be considered not a serious party. Its campaign forced the PNC to move further to the right, and probably precipitated the expulsion of its left-wing secretary Sidney King, who had pursued an increasingly bitter racial line against both Indian and white, culminating in a remarkable proposal for the partition of British Guiana (like Gaul) into three parts, one for Indians, one for Negroes and one for those who 'wish to live with other races'. King became an independent candidate and then withdrew, but the fracas undoubtedly reduced the effectiveness of the PNC's drive for Negro solidarity, even though it allowed the party to move further to the right than before.

Now, however, it was too late to make a thorough-going revision of its economic programme, and its espousal of democratic socialism of the British Labour Party type did not make an impact on the voters. It was caught by its previous emphasis on racialism and so forced to concentrate on this as the campaign progressed. The PNC fought on two fronts, the Indian-Negro fight familiar from the recent past, and the even older but now explicit black versus brown-and-white struggle, with its strong class undertones. It is not surprising that the party lost and since the UF was never a serious contender, that the PPP should gain twenty seats to the PNC's eleven, although the discrepancy in the popular vote was much narrower; in 1953 the PPP polled 51 per cent of the total vote, in 1957

47 per cent and in 1961 only 43 per cent, with the PNC taking 41 per cent[6].

The Riots of February 1962

There was much uncertainty among the electorate as the PPP assumed the considerably greater powers of the new constitution, with the prospect of essentially complete independence in the near future. There was a tendency in some circles, especially those of the large expatriate firms, to give the new Government the benefit of the doubt, but the other political parties themselves were smarting from defeat. This was especially true of the PNC, where it was justifiably feared that in the next election in four years' time the East Indian section of the electorate would be in such a strong majority that no Negro-based party would stand a chance of coming to power. The strategy which this indicated to the party was to seek the support of the middle-classes on the right, in the process hoping to destroy the base of D'Aguiar's United Force which was held to have been the main cause of the PNC's failure in the election.

The new PPP Government might have stood by while the other two parties destroyed themselves over the leadership of the Opposition; but much to its credit it embarked immediately on a fresh drive for economic development, as shown in its proposals for the 1962 Budget. Unfortunately, as we have seen, the party had not yet been able to reassure a large part of the electorate that its aims were not the immediate sovietisation of the economy. Much economic and social opinion among the creole bourgeoisie in B.G. is on about the same level as that of the radical right in the U.S.A., and such measures as State control of most of the primary schools, mild exchange control, and capital gains taxation—all features of conservative western societies—were with the aid of a largely irresponsible

[6] See *British Guiana Conference 1963* (London, H.M.S.O., Cmd. 2203, 1963), p. 7.

Press seen as portents of imminent Communism. This misinterpretation was helped by the excessive class-war content of the speeches of some of the Ministers; and there is little doubt that some party members had been encouraged by the success of Castro in Cuba, especially after the Bay of Pigs fiasco, to believe that they could bring about and sustain a similar change in the economic order in Guiana.

But if one paid attention to what the new Government actually tried to do, rather than to what some of its members said, many of the fiscal measures were quite sensible. While the programme of economic development *expenditure* was seriously open to question, at least in the essential field of deflecting resources from consumption to investment it was beginning at long last to take firm action; and in this regard it was a long way ahead of many countries in the Alliance for Progress, with their reactionary aversion from adequate taxation for development. At the least the Budget proposals constituted a definite basis for discussion, most certainly debatable on basic assumptions, but not either wildly irrelevant or unrealistic; and certainly not communistic.

They did however involve a radical departure from previous practice and this, coupled with the neurotic fear of the Communist aims of the PPP, implied that it would have been the path of wisdom for Jagan to have attempted to seek as much co-operation as possible—at least in terms of constructive opposition—in securing their passage into law. Even within his own party many of the leaders were avowedly not Marxist, especially the leaders of the wealthier rice farmers and the merchants, and it would certainly have strengthened his hand to have secured as broad-based support as possible for the urgently needed increases in economic development. He did not do so however, and the Budget proposals were not presented in a form which appealed effectively to a united effort by the whole nation.

But even granting this typical lack of political tact, there was no real basis for the storm of virulent criticism which the United Front let loose on the Budget. Mainly through the medium of his newspaper, the *Chronicle*, D'Aguiar and his followers went to extravagant lengths in their denunciations, claiming that the new taxes and savings levy seriously attacked individual freedom and would drastically reduce the workers' standard of living. A 'vindictive and malicious spirit . . . prowls through the Budget. . . . The Budget's tax reform proposals are merely the transcription of doctrinaire Marxism into the fiscal policy of this poor country', said the *Sunday Chronicle's* editorial of 4 February. In the next ten days the criticism mounted to increasingly hysterical levels, and it became clear that the UF was seizing the opportunity that the Budget had presented to force the PPP Government from power by the wave of 'popular' anger over the new taxes. By 15 February the *Daily Chronicle* was saying that 'The Government must create the climate for restoring the nation's normal life by resigning. This is the only way out— the safe way for the workers!'

At the same time the trade unions were involved in labour disputes with the Government, especially over pay and conditions for the predominantly Negro civil servants, teachers and lower-paid Government workers. This naturally brought the PNC in on their side, and the two campaigns joined together in one series of large demonstrations—confined almost entirely to Georgetown— against the elected Government. The PNC was at first reluctant to be associated wholeheartedly with the UF's anti-Budget struggle, in which many of the local shopkeepers actively encouraged and paid their workers to go out on strike, but eventually joined in for fear of not being thought sufficiently anti-Jagan and probably because it too saw a chance to topple the Government; the leaders Burnham and D'Aguiar were photographed ostentatiously shaking hands with each other, after jointly

leading an illegal procession around the Government buildings.[7]

Given the white-hot fervour that had been whipped up among the Georgetown population by the violent rhetoric of the opposition's political leaders and newspapers in the previous two weeks, and given the idleness enforced by several days of strikes in the city, it is not surprising that on Friday 16 February the tension erupted in a riot of arson, looting and violence, which killed five men and injured eighty, and destroyed property worth about $11½ million in the business centre of Georgetown. As the official *Report* emphasised (pp. 60–1) 'There is no evidence of the disturbances being the direct result of a racial conflict', but they were more in the nature of a 'spontaneous combustion when some highly fermented substance is subjected to long pressures'. Once the arson and looting had begun on a large scale, and it was clear that the firemen and the police had lost control of the situation, large sections of the Georgetown crowd joined in the general stealing, including even normally respectable members of society. In the words of a contemporary Trinidad calypso about the riot:

> A woman walk in a store on Main Street
>   Slippers on she feet,
> Durty petticoat, long-time straw hat
>   And she smellin' worse than that;
>
> But she walk out like a lady
>   High heels, glasses, jewellery,
> The straw hat she had on wearin' before
>   She take match and she burn it inside the store.[8]

---

[7] For a thorough account of the immediate events leading up to the riots, see the *Report of a Commission of Inquiry into Disturbances in British Guiana in February 1962* (London, H.M.S.O., Colonial No. 354, 1962, p. 82). A shorter account from a different viewpoint is by Janet Jagan in *Monthly Review* (New York) April 1962. The editors of this Marxist review, Paul Sweezy and Leo Huberman, in this issue give perhaps the most bizarre explanation yet seen of the riots—that it was a Central Intelligence Agency plot! While holding no brief for the CIA, I doubt that it would display the inefficiency that one would have to postulate for the riots as a cloak-and-dagger operation.

[8] From 'B.G. War', by Francisco Slinger (alias 'The Mighty Sparrow').

Only the arrival of British troops, brought in at the Government's request, restored order to the city.

The Opposition leaders, together with most of the rest of Guiana, expressed shock and sorrow at the results of their agitation. It is possible, of course, that they had not been astute enough to anticipate the probable effects of their continued disregard of public order in the previous week; in which case they were truly irresponsible. If they did anticipate such a wretched conclusion, then they were guilty of using illegal means to bring down a legally elected Government, which had in no sense begun to act dictatorially, whatever might be its plans for the future.

The Aftermath of the Riots

The alarms and excusions of the last two years have been an inevitable sequel to the riots, which showed conclusively that the elected Government could no longer effectively govern, since the creole society was no longer willing for it to do so, and the creoles controlled the capital city and much of the administration, without which the country cannot function. These riots also showed, however, that the Government was too strong in its sources of power to be brought down by unconstitutional action. They resolved nothing and apparently taught nothing, except that the situation was one of stalemate. In a typical South American state—and British Guiana *is* in South America, though it is often difficult to remember this fact—such a stalemate would have been broken by a military *coup*, since historically it has been the Army's role in such countries to take over when in its opinion the demagoguery and instability of civilian régimes threaten chaos—and often of course on even flimsier excuses. But for better or worse B.G. has no such army, and although Jagan has tried to form one (based mainly on his party's youth wingers) there is little likelihood of its coming into being effectively, certainly not with the self-appointed judicial role of a Latin American army.

Thus there is no means of resolution of the stalemate, short of a considerable change of heart by one or more of the leaders, or of the appropriate exercise of colonial power. The British Guiana Independence Conference of October 1962 broke down because the political leaders were unable to reach agreement on several important questions, especially the problems of proportional representation, of the voting age, and of whether fresh elections should be held before independence. The stalemate thus continued and the crisis was brought to a head again in April 1963, when the Opposition trade unions called a general strike over the issue of a new (and eventually abortive) labour relations Bill, under which the Government would have had the right to decide which union should be recognised by the employers in collective bargaining procedures. The general strike went on for eighty days, causing a serious and irrevocable loss of output, and although it started very peaceably inevitably drifted at the end towards violence, to counter which British troops were again called in. Only the high level of demand for Guiana's exports, caused by the world sugar shortage and brisk industrial activity in America and Europe, saved her economy from serious collapse at this time.

In July 1963 the Colonial Secretary visited Georgetown to help resolve the crisis of the general strike, and in the course of his visit called on the leaders to form a National Government; but although talks were held, there was not sufficient goodwill to allow a coalition to form, probably since each side saw an opportunity for a more complete victory in the near future. The Independence Conference reconvened in October 1963 and again the politicians were unable to reach an agreement on the previously undecided questions. This time the conference did not break down however, for on the initiative of Dr. Jagan the three leaders requested 'the British Government to settle on their authority all outstanding constitutional issues, and we undertake

to accept their decisions'.[9] Such an extraordinary request revealed quite strikingly the poverty of ideas and leadership current on all sides in Guianese politics, and also their curious dependence on the colonial power.

It cannot be said that the British Government displayed a brilliant grasp of the problems either, in the delivery of its Solomon-like judgement. While sufficiently perceptive to point out that the colony's basic troubles were political and not racial, and therefore that political solutions must be found, the detailed proposals in the Colonial Secretary's statement leave much to be desired. On the first issue, that of proportional representation, the decision went in favour of the most extreme form of P.R.—the Israeli system—which had been advocated by the United Force. The whole country is to be one constituency with each voter having one vote, and with seats being allocated to parties in proportion to the percentage of this total vote that each gains. There is to be no minimum percentage of the poll which any party must win in order to be considered for the allocation of seats; thus a party winning only two per cent of the vote would secure two per cent of the seats.

It is clear that this formula will make for a proliferation of splinter parties each catering for special interests, and will result in a weak Government, though it cannot be denied that weak government is what B.G. has had for several years. The official hope is that the much easier path to political influence if not power opened up by the new formula will attract new blood (or recall disenchanted old blood) into Guianese politics, and thus give a chance for new ideas and abilities. This may come about; it is also possible that since each minor group can have its own representation, the society will find its many divisions increasing, to the detriment of that process of integration of the society to which we have called attention. The decision also appears to reward the extremely unconstitutional action taken in recent

[9] *British Guiana Conference 1963* (London, H.M.S.O. Cmd. 2203, 1963), p. 4.

years by the Opposition, especially the UF, and will tend to
encourage the more extreme elements of the PPP to think
that they also by similar action can sway the Colonial Office
to take account of their views.[10] We are already seeing some
evidence of this in the current (March-April 1964) crop of
arson and murder, this time being waged mainly by the
PPP sugar trade union, in a bid to establish ascendancy
over the opposition Man Power Citizens Association.

The other decisions by the British Government were
firstly, not to put the voting age down from 21 to 18 as
Dr. Jagan requested, which would have improved the
chances of the faster-growing young East Indian electorate;
and secondly, to insist on elections before independence.
These were both sensible decisions, given the drastic
change in the electoral system, but the effectiveness of the
latter was greatly reduced by Mr. Sandys' refusal to give
a firm date for independence after the elections, although
it was fairly clear that such a date was an implicit condition
in the tripartite request to him, which stated that 'further
discussions between ourselves would therefore serve no
useful purpose and would result only in further delaying
British Guiana's independence and in continued uncertainty
in the country'. The fixing of the date Mr. Sandys left
for a post-election conference.

It is not surprising that both Dr. Jagan and Mr. Burnham
took great exception to this refusal, though Burnham's
public chagrin at this must surely be greatly tempered in
private by the opportunity held out to the PNC by the new
voting system. Although a skilled politician would have
anticipated the possibility of such an unfavourable set of
decisions from Britain, Dr. Jagan apparently did not do so
and in his anger he 'repudiated' the British proposals,
thus going back on his agreement to abide by the arbitra-
tion; but in practice such repudiation can mean little
except a refusal to co-operate with the colonial authorities

[10] See a letter to *The Times* of 3 April 1964 by Lawrence Mann, until
very recently a Parliamentary Secretary in the PPP Government.

in implementing the new electoral and constitutional proposals.

Although the Colonial Secretary promised that the 'constitutional documents . . . required to give effect to the decisions which I have outlined will be drafted without delay', there has in fact been a considerable delay in arranging for the new electoral system, and it seems most unlikely that elections can be held much before the end of 1964.[11] This long waiting period has meant a chance both for the opponents of the Sandys judgement (the PPP) and its supporters (the PNC and the UF) to recover from the shock and to organise their responses. It is unlikely that these responses will make for a peaceful pre-electoral or electoral campaign, and we may yet see violence on a greater scale than ever before during the coming summer.

It is important to be clear about the issues presently at stake in British Guiana. Her past history has been such that no democratic Government that was not markedly socialist could have come to power in the last few years. Such administrations have a tendency to drift rightwards as they stay in power, but in any event they would have had to start out as radical. It would be wrong to believe that a programme less socialist than, say, the more radical wing of the British Labour Party would have commanded electoral support.

Many people in the West, especially in the United States worry about a 'Communist take-over'. To the extent that they think about this phrase at all, these people probably mean the possibility that Guiana might be used as a Soviet base. Since Cuba already fills this role much better, being close to the United States, larger and more viable, more racially homogenous and—most important of all for penetration purposes—an integral part of *Latin* America, this possibility seems remote. It might have some use to the Russians as purely nuisance value, but considerations

[11] The target date at the time of writing was October.

of geography seem to preclude any more serious role; on the other hand, if the Soviet-Chinese conflict develops, perhaps it could be useful as a base for Chinese penetration of Latin America, which in turn would stimulate Russian interest.

But this is merely fanciful speculation; the danger in British Guiana is far more serious and immediate than the small risk of a 'take-over'. It is simply the prospect of breakdown of any effective government at all.

V. CONCLUSION

It is difficult to escape the conclusion that the British Government is rather bored with British Guiana, and indeed perhaps with the British Caribbean as a whole. The rather casual approach taken at the last Independence Conference suggests that there is a disposition to leave this particular backwater to the American hegemony, rather as almost a century ago Lord Derby remarked that 'The natural market of the West Indies [is] America not Europe.'

Yet there would be a grave forfeiture of responsibility if Britain were to wash its hands of this area, for it is—to a degree far exceeding that of most of the rest of the Commonwealth—our *creation*. It is impossible to live in former British possessions in Africa and in Asia without feeling that the colonial era was, for good or ill, simply an episode in their long history, and that soon this episode will be forgotten; and equally impossible to live in the West Indies without realising that they are quite different societies, amalgams of Europeans, Africans and Asians assembled in America to produce sugar and other tropical crops for a once urgent metropolitan demand; and now, having fulfilled this role, packed off into 'independence' with a paltry golden handshake, a throttling down of immigration from their shores, and a sigh of relief.

It must be the task of a fresh approach to this area—and it is possible that with a new British Government this might come about—to devise a new form of political and economic relationship that would preserve and extend the spirit of independence and self-respect in these ex-colonies, while at the same time giving them the prospect of an adequate and stable reward for their hard work and enterprise. It will take some ingenuity to do this, and Britain has not been particularly adept in recent years at the invention of new political and economic institutions;

a joint approach both with the other European nations who have influence in the Caribbean and with the North American countries might prove fruitful, although one would need to dispel the mistrust left over from the days of the old Caribbean Commission.

Without more active and generous participation by Britain, the economic and social future of these countries of our invention could well be bleak, and nowhere more so than in British Guiana, whose struggle to forge an economy and a society out of the thoughtless colonial assembling of plantation labour from so many disparate sources I have tried to analyse in this book.

POSTSCRIPT

This book was completed early in April 1964, when the strike of the PPP-supported sugar workers' trade union was still in its early stages. Since then the bitterness it has engendered, plus the political manoeuvring that has occurred in anticipation of the new electoral rules, have resulted in tensions erupting in quite unprecedented violence. By the time the strike ended in late July, some 160 Guianese of all races had lost their lives, many of them innocent women and children, victims of indiscriminate arson and bombings; over one thousand houses have been destroyed and about two per cent of the population forced to live as refugees. Bitterness has become so deep that there have been serious proposals from Indians in Berbice to partition the country into racial areas.

Without first-hand knowledge of the country during this period of horror it would be pointless and indeed presumptuous to comment in any detail. While it was only to be expected that this pre-election period would see much more violence than hitherto, the pace of the dissolution of the society has been surprising. It would appear that the political leaders, who for so long have been unable—at the cost of many lives—to put the national interest and common humanity above their own ambitions, are now beginning to lose control of their more extreme followers. In this situation the measures taken by the new Governor, Sir Richard Luyt —although in their threats of flogging and life imprisonment both too severe and not realistic—may have stabilised a runaway situation.

But it is clear that the present situation is not stable at all in the longer run, and until leadership of much higher quality is displayed in all parties, the Guianese seem condemned to a miserable life of suspicion and stagnation. Dr. Eric Williams, the Premier of Trinidad, after trying at

great length and in vain to bring the present leaders together, has proposed a solution (at the Commonwealth Prime
Ministers' Conference of July 1964) that apparently involves
a kind of United Nations trusteeship for a limited time until
things can return more nearly to normal and the forces of
integration—which even in the present disturbances have
still been at work—have time to assert themselves as the
dominant characteristic in the society. There is much merit
in these proposals, though perhaps it would be preferable if
the problem could be solved by joint action within the
Commonwealth, since the United Nations has already a
very great deal to cope with from its limited resources.
A successful Commonwealth solution to the Guianese
problem could indeed be a triumphal test of this multi-
racial grouping of nations.

August 1964.

Oxford University Press, Amen House, London E.C.4

GLASGOW NEW YORK TORONTO MELBOURNE WELLINGTON
BOMBAY CALCUTTA MADRAS KARACHI LAHORE DACCA
CAPE TOWN SALISBURY NAIROBI IBADAN ACCRA
KUALA LUMPUR HONG KONG

Printed in Great Britain by R. J. Acford Ltd., Chichester

BRITISH GUIANA

Problems of Cohesion in an
Immigrant Society

PETER NEWMAN

Issued under the auspices of the
Institute of Race Relations, London

OXFORD UNIVERSITY PRESS

LONDON   NEW YORK

1964

BRITISH GUIANA